PILLARS OF RUSSIA'S DISINFORMATION AND PROPAGANDA ECOSYSTEM (ANNOTATED)

By the Global Engagement Center,
US Department of State

Foreword by Slava Suwarrow

Additional materials provided by
the AI Editorial Board at Nimble Books LLC

FOREWORD

What a unique and important topic! The successful promotion of Russian disinformation, propaganda, and false narratives around the world is one of the Kremlin's most effective tools for undermining democracy and furthering its own interests. And it does so without leaving a trace. This book provides essential insights into how this disinformation machine works, as well as how to counteract it.

The State Department's Global Engagement Center holds many of the world's foremost experts Russian disinformation. They have written extensively about the role of disinformation in Russia's hybrid warfare strategy, as well as its impact on our understanding of Russian politics and culture. Their work is indispensable if we want to understand not only what lies behind the Kremlin's campaigns but also how to defeat them.

So let me congratulate everyone at GEC once again on the 2020 publication of this report book–it remains both timely and essential reading for anyone interested in understanding modern Russia, its malign influence, and the ways we can counter it.

Slava Suwarrow
Kyiv, 2022

U.S. DEPARTMENT of STATE

GEC Special Report:

Pillars of Russia's Disinformation and Propaganda Ecosystem

August 2020

Table of Contents

Introduction

Understanding Russia's Disinformation and Propaganda Ecosystem

As the U.S. Government's dedicated center for countering foreign disinformation and propaganda, the Global Engagement Center (GEC) at the U.S. Department of State has a mandate to expose and counter threats from malign actors that utilize these tactics. In this field, Russia continues to be a leading threat. The Department works with interagency and global partners to meet this challenge, with the GEC playing a key role in coordinating efforts and helping lead a global response.

A central part of this effort is exposing Russia's tactics so that partner and allied governments, civil society organizations, academia, the press, and the international public can conduct further analysis of their own and thereby increase collective resilience to disinformation and propaganda.

In line with that goal, this report draws on publicly available reporting to provide an overview of Russia's disinformation and propaganda ecosystem. Russia's disinformation and propaganda ecosystem is the collection of official, proxy, and unattributed communication channels and platforms that Russia uses to create and amplify false narratives. The ecosystem consists of five main pillars: official government communications, state-funded global messaging, cultivation of proxy sources, weaponization of social media, and cyber-enabled disinformation. The Kremlin bears direct responsibility for cultivating these tactics and platforms as part of its approach to using information as a weapon. It invests massively in its

> "Russia's disinformation and propaganda ecosystem is the collection of official, proxy, and unattributed communication channels and platforms that Russia uses to create and amplify false narratives."

propaganda channels, its intelligence services and its proxies to conduct malicious cyber activity to support their disinformation efforts, and it leverages outlets that masquerade as news sites or research institutions to spread these false and misleading narratives. This report also focuses specific attention on Russia's tactic of leveraging proxy voices that proliferate pro-Kremlin disinformation and propaganda. It includes profiles on a cross section of outlets playing this role within the broader ecosystem, and it explains how they serve as critical connective tissue to the other pillars within the broader ecosystem.

The GEC has developed the "ecosystem" concept and has broken the ecosystem down into five pillars as a way to contextualize the threat posed by Russia in this field. A common understanding is a necessary prerequisite to developing analytical tools to monitor the various threat vectors and crafting the policies and procedures that allow for countermeasures. While this effort continues, the issuance of this report aims to heighten awareness of the threat posed by disinformation and further the international dialogue among the nations, organizations, and individuals who are committed to countering these malign efforts.

The disinformation and propaganda ecosystem that Russia continues to cultivate does not stand unopposed. A thriving counter-disinformation community comprised of governments, civil society, academia, the press, the private sector, and citizens around the world who refuse to tolerate these tactics is pushing back. This report is offered by the U.S. Department of State as a contribution to these joint efforts.

Background

In any analysis of Russia's disinformation and propaganda tactics, it is important to note there are multiple terms and concepts that have been used to describe the nature of this threat. "Information Confrontation" is the term used in Russian strategic and military circles to describe their approach to the use of information in both peacetime and conflict. There is also a rich public record of the use of "Active Measures" to describe long-standing Russian political warfare methods that utilize disinformation and propaganda as a core tool. These concepts speak to Russia's strategic formulation that it is in a state of perpetual conflict with its perceived adversaries.

Russia's current disinformation and propaganda operations are an integrated tactical manifestation of this strategic view. Analyzing this approach in a manner that increases resiliency begins with a recognition that there is no single media platform where propaganda and disinformation are distributed. Nor is there uniformity of messages among different sources.

Rather, Russia has operationalized the concept of perpetual adversarial competition in the information environment by encouraging the development of a disinformation and propaganda ecosystem that allows for varied and overlapping approaches that reinforce each other even when individual messages within the system appear contradictory. This ecosystem reflects both the sources of disinformation and propaganda—official government statements, state-funded media outlets, proxy websites, bots, false social media personas, cyber-enabled disinformation operations, etc.—and the different tactics that these channels use.

Russia's willingness to employ this approach provides it with three perceived advantages. First, it allows for the introduction of numerous variations of the same false narratives. This allows for the different pillars of the ecosystem to fine tune their disinformation narratives to suit different target audiences because there is no need for consistency, as there would be with attributed government communications. Second, it provides plausible deniability for Kremlin officials when proxy sites peddle blatant and dangerous disinformation, allowing them to deflect criticism while still introducing pernicious information. Third, it creates a media multiplier effect among the different pillars of the ecosystem that boost their reach and resonance.

The media multiplier effect can, at times, create disinformation storms with potentially dangerous effects for those Russia perceives as adversaries at the international, national, and local level. In the past, Russia has leveraged this dynamic to shield itself from criticism for its involvement in malign activity. This approach also allows Russia to be opportunistic, such as with COVID-19, where it has used the global pandemic as a hook to push longstanding disinformation and propaganda narratives.

This ecosystem approach is also well-suited to reinforce Russia's general aims of questioning the value of democratic institutions, and of weakening the international credibility and international cohesion of the United States and its allies and partners. Because some pillars of this ecosystem generate their own momentum, as opposed to waiting for specific orders from the Kremlin on every occasion, they can be responsive to distinct policy goals or developing situations, and then pivot back to their status quo of generally pouring scorn on Russia's perceived adversaries.

The perpetual conflict that Russia sees in the information environment also means that officials and state media may take one side of an issue, while outlets with a measure of independence will adopt their own variations on similar overarching false narratives. The ecosystem approach is fitting for this dynamic because it does not require harmonization among the different pillars. By simultaneously furthering multiple versions of a given story, these actors muddy the waters of the information environment in order to confuse those trying to discern the truth.

The Report

This report provides a visual representation of the ecosystem described above, as well as an example of the media multiplier effect it enables. This serves to demonstrate how the different pillars of the ecosystem play distinct roles and feed off of and bolster each other.

The report also includes brief profiles of select proxy sites and organizations that occupy an intermediate role between the pillars of the ecosystem with clear links to Russia and those that are meant to be fully deniable. The emphasis on these proxy sites is meant to highlight the important role they play, which can be overlooked given the attention paid to official Russian voices on one end of the spectrum, and the social media manipulation and cyber-enabled threats on the other.

Disclaimer: The GEC cannot vouch for the security of the sites cited within this report.

GEC | PILLARS OF RUSSIA'S DISINFORMATION
AND PROPAGANDA ECOSYSTEM

Global Engagement Center

Official Government Communications

- Kremlin or Ministry statement[1]
- Official Russian social media post[2]
- Statement or quote by Russian official[3]

State-Funded Global Messaging

- State-funded, foreign-facing media[4]
- State-funded, domestic-facing media[5]
- Foreign-based, Russian state-funded media[6]
- International Russian socio-cultural institutions[7]

Cultivation of Proxy Sources

- Russia-aligned outlets with global reach[8]
- Local language-specific outlets[9]
- Witting proliferators of Russian narratives[10]
- Unwitting proliferators of Russian narratives[11]
- Foreign state narrative amplification[12]

Weaponization of Social Media

- Infiltration of domestic conversations[13]
- Standing campaigns to undermine faith in institutions[14]
- Amplification of protests or civil discord[15]

Cyber-Enabled Disinformation

- Hack & Release[16]
- Site capture[17]
- Cloned websites[18]
- Forgeries[19]
- Disruption of official sources or objective media[20]

VISIBLE

CONNECTION TO RUSSIA

OBSCURED

DENIED

 **GEC**
Global Engagement Center

Endnotes

Official Government Communications

Kremlin or Ministry statement
- AP: Russia claims US running secret bio weapons lab in Georgia
- TASS: Neither Soviet Union, nor Russia perform research codenamed Novichok - diplomat
- MFA Russia: Publications in Arab media regarding Russian nationals' involvement in the military operations in Libya
- TASS: Russian Foreign Ministry slams flimsy MH17 accusations of JIT

Official Russian social media post
- Russian Embassy in UK Twitter: The [Skripal] incident appears to be yet another crooked attempt by the UK authorities to discredit Russia.
- Russian Embassy in Malaysia Facebook.
- Russian Foreign Ministry Facebook: Revisionist History Regarding the Baltic Forest Brothers

Statement or quote by senior Russian official
- Rossiya 24: MFA Spokeswoman Maria Zakharova claims that Osama bin Laden was welcomed at the White House
- MFA Russia Facebook page: Russian Rep to EU article in the EUObserver citing Dulles Plan

State-Funded Global Messaging

State-funded, foreign-facing media
- Sputnik Mundo: COVID-19 Brings Attention to US Secret Laboratories on the Borders of Russia and China
- Sputnik Czech: COVID-19 mutation may be due to 5G
- RT Arabic: Washington accuses Moscow of 'collusion with Assad in support of Haftar'
- RT: Int'l investigators allowed Ukraine to fabricate MH17 evidence – Russia
- Sputnik: Wicked Games: US 'Uses Terrorism as Main Mechanism of Its Foreign Policy'

State-funded, domestic-facing media
- RIA Novosti: Source: Johnson will be put on an artificial lung ventilation machine
- Perviy Kanal: The "Vremya" news program alleged President Trump's connection to COVID-19
- Rossiya 24: Vesti Nedeli, the flagship weekly news analysis program, cited fabricated documents to falsely claim Alexei Navalniy was a CIA agent.

Foreign-based, Russian state-funded media
- LINX: The pro-Moscow media (Moldova)
- Coda Story: Russia, The New power in Central Africa (para. 6, 10-11)

International Russian socio-cultural institutions
- Atlantic Council: "The Long Arm of Russian "Soft" Power"
- Ponars Eurasia: "Russia's Anti-American Propaganda in the Euromaidan Era"
- The Foreign Policy Centre: "The non-governmental sector: Pro-Russia tools masquerading as independent voices"

Cultivation of Proxy Sources

Russia-aligned outlets with global reach
- Global Research: COVID-19: Further Evidence that the Virus Originated in the U.S.
- Strategic Culture Foundation: The Facts About Crimea Should Be Recognised, And So Should Crimea
- News Front: How karma works: is it possible that COVID-19 is a successful project of the USA?

Local language-specific outlets
- Hlavne Spravy (Slovakia): Why They Hate Russia in the West
- Compact Magazine (Germany): Vladimir Putin: Talk to the Germans

Witting proliferators of Russian narratives
- The Moscow Times: 'Hybrid Truth': Russia-Linked Italians Sing Praises for Moscow's Virus Aid
- Anton Shekhovtsov: Russia and the Western Far Right: Tango Noir
- Investigation uncovers Dutch politician's ties to Russia

Unwitting proliferators of Russian narratives
- NATO: The "Lisa Case:" Germany as a target of Russian disinformation (last para. 'Russian Networks' section)
- United States Department of Justice: Report On The Investigation Into Russian Interference In The 2016 Presidential Election (pg. 14-15)

Foreign state narrative amplification
- FPRI: Iranian, Chinese and Russian Overt Media on Coronavirus
- EEAS: EEAS Special Report Update: Short Assessment of Narratives and Disinformation Around the COVID-19 Pandemic (Update 23 April - 18 May)

Weaponization of Social Media

Infiltration of domestic conversations
- U.S. Senate Select Committee on Intelligence: Russian Active Measures Campaigns and Interference in the 2016 U.S. Election. Volume 2: Russia's Use of Social Media with Additional Views
- El Pais: Russian network used Venezuelan accounts to deepen Catalan crisis

Standing campaigns to inflame domestic discord & undermine faith in institutions
- International Centre for Defence and Security: Contemporary Deterrence: Lessons and Insights From Enhanced Forward Presence (pg. 12-13)
- Computational Propaganda Project: The IRA, Social Media and Political Polarization in the United States, 2012-2018

Russian-instigated or amplified protests
- U.S. Department of Justice: United States v. Internet Research Agency LLC et al. (pgs. 20-23)
- Bloomberg: France to Probe Possible Russian Influence on Yellow Vest Riots

Cyber-Enabled Disinformation

Hack & Release
- United States Department of Justice: Report On The Investigation Into Russian Interference In The 2016 Presidential Election (pgs. 38-48)
- Government of the Netherlands: Netherlands Defence Intelligence and Security Service disrupts Russian cyber operation targeting OPCW

Site Capture
- EU Monitor: "Protecting Europe from large scale cyber-attacks and disruptions: enhancing preparedness, (See Annex 18)
- Reuters: Georgia, backed by U.S. and Britain, Blames Russia for 'Paralyzing' Cyber Attack

Cloned Websites
- FireEye: APT28: A Window into Russia's Cyber Espionage Operations? (pgs. 11, 13-14)
- New York Times: The Agency (see para. 6: clones of Louisiana news sites)
- Heinrich Böll Stiftung: Finland's Reluctance to Join NATO (see para. 10; clone of Hybrid CoE site)

Forgeries
- NPR: Anti-Doping Agency Bans Russia From International Sports Events For 4 Years
- Bellingcat: Comparison of Digital Globe 17 July Satellite Imagery with Russian Ministry of Defense 17 July Satellite Imagery

Disruption of official sources or objective media
- Reuters: Georgia, backed by U.S. and Britain, Blames Russia for 'Paralyzing' Cyber Attack
- Symantec: WastedLocker: Symantec Identifies Wave of Attacks Against U.S. Organizations

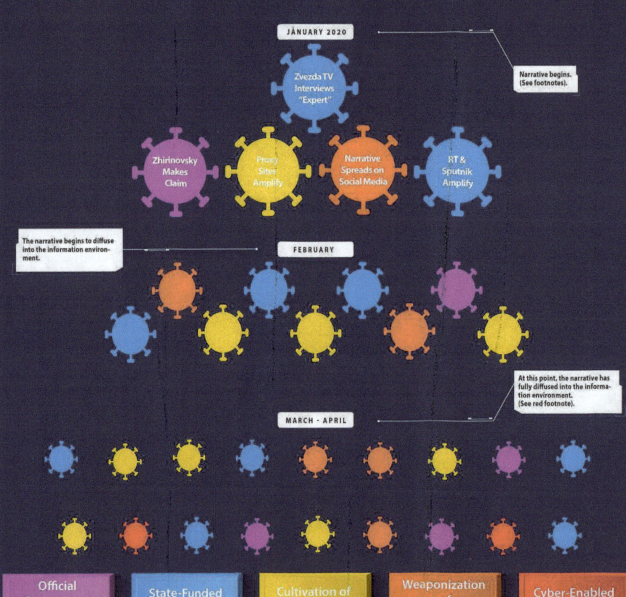

Preface for the Proxy Site Profiles

The following profiles focus on some of the proxy outlets and institutions that proliferate Russia's disinformation and propaganda narratives. As the report notes, some of the individuals and institutions behind these sites benefit greatly from an association with the Kremlin. Others strive to maintain a veneer of separation from Russia, but as our research and analysis show, they serve no other purpose but to push pro-Kremlin content.

The GEC's goal in detailing the nature of these outlets is twofold: to promote a more complete understanding of how these outlets operate as an informal network; and to demonstrate how content produced and amplified by these sites enables the proliferation of disinformation and propaganda across other pillars of the ecosystem.

This collection of profiles is not meant to be exhaustive, nor does it reflect any sort of prioritization or ranking. Rather, it is a select cross section drawn from a multitude of similar operations and is meant to provide a broad representation of the type of outlets that Russia has cultivated to play an important role in its larger disinformation and propaganda ecosystem.

They cover various geographies and have their own target audiences, though there is considerable overlap between some of them largely due to their online presence. While sharing similar practices, they have each developed their own styles. In a few cases, these outlets have published or republished articles authored by false personas attributed by Facebook to Russian military intelligence.

Highlights from the Proxy Site Profiles

The Strategic Culture Foundation

The *Strategic Culture Foundation* is an online journal registered in Russia that is directed by Russia's Foreign Intelligence Service (SVR) and closely affiliated with the Russian Ministry of Foreign Affairs.[1] One of its core tactics is to publish Western fringe thinkers and conspiracy theorists, giving them a broader platform, while trying to obscure the Russian origins of the journal. This tactic helps the site appear to be an organic voice within its target audience of Westerners.

Global Research

Global Research is a Canadian website that has become deeply enmeshed in Russia's broader disinformation and propaganda ecosystem. Its large roster of fringe authors and conspiracy theorists serves as a talent pool for Russian and Chinese websites. Its publications also provide a Western voice that other elements of the ecosystem can leverage to their advantage.

New Eastern Outlook

New Eastern Outlook is a pseudo-academic publication of the Russian Academy of Science's Institute of Oriental Studies that promotes disinformation and propaganda focused primarily on the Middle East, Asia, and Africa. It combines pro-Kremlin views of Russian academics with anti-U.S. views of Western fringe voices and conspiracy theorists. *New Eastern Outlook* appears to want to benefit from the veneer of respectability offered by the Russian academics it features, while also obscuring its links to state-funded institutions.

News Front

News Front is a Crimea-based disinformation and propaganda outlet with the self-proclaimed goal of providing an "alternative source of information" for Western audiences. With reported ties to the Russian security services and Kremlin funding, it is particularly focused on supporting Russia-backed forces in Ukraine. *News Front*'s manipulative tactics to boost reach led to a near total dismantling of its presence on social media in early 2020.

Highlights from the Proxy Site Profiles

SouthFront

SouthFront: Analysis and Intelligence (a.k.a. *SouthFront*), is a multilingual online disinformation site registered in Russia that focuses on military and security issues. With flashy infographics, maps, and videos, *SouthFront* combines Kremlin talking points with detailed knowledge of military systems and ongoing conflicts. It attempts to appeal to military enthusiasts, veterans, and conspiracy theorists, all while going to great lengths to hide its connections to Russia.

Katehon

Katehon is a Moscow-based quasi-think-tank that is a proliferator of virulent anti-Western disinformation and propaganda via its website, which is active in five languages. It is led by individuals with clear links to the Russian state and the Russian intelligence services. Within Russia's broader disinformation and propaganda ecosystem, *Katehon* plays the role of providing supposedly independent, analytical material aimed largely at European audiences, with content allegedly dedicated to "the creation and defense of a secure, democratic and just international system".

Geopolitica.ru

Geopolitica.ru serves as a platform for Russian ultra-nationalists to spread disinformation and propaganda targeting Western and other audiences. Inspired by the Eurasianist ideology of the Russian philosopher and Eurasian imperialist Alexander Dugin, *Geopolitica.ru* views itself as caught in a perpetual information war against the Western ideals of democracy and liberalism. The website's cooperation with other outlets in Russia's disinformation and propaganda ecosystem broadens the reach of its messaging, which seeks to destabilize and weaken Western institutions.

Proxy Site Profiles

The Strategic Culture Foundation

An article on Strategic Culture Foundation's website promoting Russia's version of history.

Summary

The *Strategic Culture Foundation* is an online journal registered in Russia, directed by Russia's Foreign Intelligence Service (SVR), and closely affiliated with the Russian Ministry of Foreign Affairs. The outlet plays a central role among a group of linked websites that proliferate Russian disinformation and propaganda.[2] One of its core tactics is to attract authors who are Western fringe thinkers and conspiracy theorists, giving them a broader platform and obscuring the Russian origins of the journal. This tactic helps the site appear to be an organic voice within its target audience of Westerners.

Introduction

The *Strategic Culture Foundation* (SCF) online journal is a prime example of long-standing Russian tactics to conceal direct state involvement in disinformation and propaganda outlets, and to cultivate local voices to serve as surrogate messengers. SCF finds obscure Western fringe thinkers and conspiracy theorists and gives their typically virulent anti-Western and anti-U.S. views a broad international platform. It does this while giving the misleading impression SCF is independent and unaffiliated with the Russian government.

This approach has several advantages for Russia:

- it gives increased circulation to what would otherwise be fringe voices that suit Russian propaganda goals;
- Russia deflects responsibility by obscuring its sponsorship of the site; and
- the individuals and conspiracy theorists they publish communicate in local idioms and understand their home audiences well.

The *Strategic Culture Foundation* and the Russian State

SCF was founded in 2005.[3] Originally it only published its journal in Russian. In September 2010, the online journal began to also appear in English.[4] This marked SCF's debut as an instrument for disinformation and propaganda on the international stage.

While SCF's online journal makes every effort to appear independent, it is directed by Russia's Foreign Intelligence Service (SVR) and closely affiliated with the Russian Ministry of Foreign Affairs.[5] There is no mention of this affiliation on SCF's English-language website, nor of any link to Russia—including the fact that SCF publishes in Russian.[6] However, International Affairs, the flagship journal of the Russian Ministry of Foreign Affairs since 1922, states on its website that SCF is its partner.[7]

SCF's president is Yuri Prokofiev, who was Moscow Party Chief from 1989 to 1991 and a Soviet Politburo Member.[8] Prokofiev is also one of the founders of the "Russian Organization for Assistance to Special Services and Law Enforcement Authorities" (ROSSPO).[9] According to its website, ROSSPO works closely with Russian security services to support the policies of the Russian state, facilitate cooperation between state institutions and civil society, and ensure the social protection of the employees of intelligence services and law enforcement authorities.[10]

SCF's Director General is Vladimir Maximenko, who is also the director of the no-longer active Russian Unity Foundation, which was focused on promoting a "positive image of Russia and Russian culture abroad," especially among the so-called Russian compatriots.[11]

Western Authors on SCF's Website

While SCF made some efforts to attract Western authors when it launched its English-language website in 2010, its writers for years were mostly Russians. This is demonstrated by the preponderance of Russian-authored articles posted on the 2 May 2015 SCF homepage.[12] Some examples include:

- Yuri Rubtsov (two articles)
- Pyotr Iskenderov
- Dmitry Minin
- Nil Nikandrov
- Nikolai Bobkin
- Alexander Donetsky (two articles)
- Natalia Meden
- Valentin Katasonov

By comparison, on that same day only three non-Russian authors, including Finian Cunningham and Pepe Escobar, had articles published on SCF homepage. Five years later, the English version of SCF's online journal has undergone a transformation. On the current SCF homepage, the Russian authors have disappeared—replaced by Westerners, although Cunningham and Escobar still remain.[13]

Finian Cunningham, who is originally from Belfast and has a background in agricultural chemistry, is the second-most prolific author for SCF, publishing more than 550 articles since 2012.[14] In one SCF article, he refers to the United States as a "lawless rogue state."[15] His other SCF articles include:

- Give North Korea some respect[16]
- Putin Stands Out as a Real World Leader[17]
- Washington Choreographing All-Out War with Russia?[18]
- The Year US-led Capitalism Became Exposed as Root of Global Conflict.[19]

Cunningham's work also appears frequently on major Russian state-media outlets RT (237 results), *Sputnik* (330 results), and *RIA Novosti* (30 results).[20] [Article counts compiled on 9 June 2020.]

Retired Russian Colonel Andrei Akulov is the third most-published author on SCF's English-language website; however, his most recent article is from 2018. Similarly, longtime SCF Russian authors like Dmitry Minin, Valentin Katasonov, Pyotr Iskenderov, and Alexander Mezyaev are still published on the Russian-language website, but they stopped appearing on the English-language website in 2017 or 2018.

Some of the current Western authors on SCF's English site are:

- Brian Cloughley, a former Australian defense attaché in Pakistan who has authored 243 articles.[21] Two of his most recent are: "The Facts About Crimea Should Be Recognised, And So Should Crimea" and "Washington Wants an Arctic Circle of Confrontation."[22]

- Matthew Ehret, one of the newest Western SCF authors, has written 94 articles since April 2019.[23] He is the founder of the *Canadian Patriot Review* and the Director of the Rising Tide Foundation.[24] Besides being an author for SCF, he also writes for other disinformation sites in Russia's ecosystem, including *Oriental Review* and *Geopolitica.ru*.[25] Ehret and the *Canadian Patriot Review* are also ardent advocates of China's Belt and Road Initiative, which they see as a "force for global progress, poverty eradication, and peace."[26]

- Cynthia Chung, President of the Rising Tide Foundation, is another new SCF author, writing 15 articles since October 2019. One of her recent articles is "A 70-Year War on 'Propaganda' Built by the CIA."[27]

Russian Authors Removed from English-Language Site

SCF has tried to make its English-language site seem entirely disconnected from Russia. As noted above, when it launched its current format in 2010, it combined the writings of Russian academics with Westerners, most of whom were those with fringe views or were conspiracy theorists. The inclusion of Russian academics was likely aimed at giving the online journal the appearance of academic respectability, although most of the Russian academics also took strong anti-Western positions.

For example, a frequent author through 2018, Moscow State Institute of International Finance professor Valentin Katasonov, wrote an article entitled, "Anglo-American Money Owners Organized World War II."[28] He argued:

> The war was not unleashed by frenzied Fuhrer who happened to be ruling Germany at the time. WWII is a project created by world oligarchy or Anglo-American "money owners". Using such instruments as the US Federal Reserve System and the Bank of England they started to prepare for the next world conflict of global scale right after WWI. The USSR was the target.

Another prolific author through 2017 was Pyotr Iskenderov, senior researcher for the Institute for Slavic Studies at the Russian Academy of Sciences.[29] Some of his articles included:

- Modern Nazism as the Driving Force of Euro-Atlantic Integration[30]

- [The Czech Republic: Doomed without Russia](#)[31]
- [Estonia: Doomed Without Russia](#)[32]
- [Russia has enough gas for everyone](#)[33]
- [Brussels and Kiev: a duo of blackmailers](#)[34]

Iskenderov and Katasonov continue to write for the Russian-language version of SCF website, although they disappeared from the English-language version in 2017 and 2018, respectively.

Building a Disinformation Network

In 2010 and 2011, SCF formed explicit partnerships with *Global Research*, a Canadian website detailed in a separate paper in this report, and *The 4th Media*, an obscure, newly formed Chinese website in English that described itself as "an independent media organization based in Beijing."[35] Fringe voices and conspiracy theorists that had previously appeared on *Global Research* soon began to be published by SCF and *The 4th Media*, broadening the reach of their anti-Western views.

Cross-Fertilization Within the Network

- *Global Research* has served as a source of "talent" for SCF, *The 4th Media*, and *The 21st Century*. In the first ten years of its operation between 2001 and 2011, *Global Research* developed a large pool of authors from which other websites could draw. The three currently operational websites—SCF, *Global Research*, and *The 21st Century* (a successor website to *The 4th Media*) —appear to have formed a sub-network within the broader array of disinformation and propaganda sites, although their connections have now been obscured.

- SCF: from September 2010 through 8 March 2018, *Global Research* and *The 4th Media* were listed as its partners or at the bottom of its homepage. On 14 March 2018, no websites were listed.

- *Global Research*: From 22 September 2012 through 17 February 2018, its "Partner Websites" included SCF and *The 4th Media*. On 18 February 2018, *The 21st Century* replaced *The 4th Media* on the *Global Research* website as its only opinion website "partner."

- *The 4th Media*: From 5 August 2011 through 4 March 2019, *Global Research* and SCF were always among the preferred websites listed on its website. Now, *The 21st Century* has no links to other websites.

The reason for this apparently collaborative move to obscure the mutual ties within the network is unclear, but public reporting may have played a role. For further discussion on this topic, see the *Global Research* profile in this report.

Strategic Culture Foundation's Social Media Platforms as of June 2020

Platform	Language	Engagement
Facebook	English	28,182 followers
	Russian	13,187 followers
Twitter	English	dormant since 2019; active once on 8 May 2020
	Russian	218 followers; dormant since 2019
YouTube	English	491 subscribers
VKontakte	Russian	2,590 followers

Proxy Site Profiles

New Eastern Outlook

Screenshot of an article on New Eastern Outlook's website that promotes Russia's version of the Skripal poisoning.

Summary

New Eastern Outlook is a pseudo-academic publication of the Russian Academy of Science's Institute of Oriental Studies that promotes disinformation and propaganda focused primarily on the Middle East, Asia, and Africa. It combines pro-Kremlin views of Russian academics with anti-U.S. views of Western fringe voices and conspiracy theorists. *New Eastern Outlook's* English-language website does not clearly state that it is a product of the Institute. The site appears to want to benefit from the veneer of respectability offered by the Russian academics it features, while also obscuring its links to state-funded institutions.

Introduction

The online journal *New Eastern Outlook* (NEO) first appeared in 2013. Its association with the Russian Academy of Science's Institute of Oriental Studies is not mentioned in NEO's About Us page.[36] The logo of the Institute of Oriental Studies with Cyrillic letters (at left) does appear at the bottom of the NEO homepage. It is hyper-linked to the Russian language website of the Institute without any explanation of the connection between the two, even in Russian. The image and link to the website is the only sign of a connection between the organizations visible to visitors of the NEO English language site. Confirmation of the links between them can be found on the Institute's website, where NEO is listed as one of its periodical publications.[37]

NEO's Partners

NEO lists four "partners" on its homepage.[38] None are academic institutions or academics--all are Western conspiracy theorists, fringe groups, or fringe thinkers. One NEO partner has a long history of endorsing bizarre anti-Semitic conspiracy theories while another has written glowingly about North Korea.

NEO's Western Authors

The Western authors published by NEO write highly anti-U.S. anti-Western articles. One such author, Canadian Christopher Black, has written 118 articles for NEO starting in November 2014.[39] In February 2020, he described a U.S. military exercise with NATO allies as a prelude to an attack on Russia, writing:

> I have written several times about the continuing NATO preparations for an attack on Russia, a second Operation Barbarossa, the code name for the Nazi invasion of the USSR in 1941. Circumstances prompt me to write about it again, for as of the last week in January the Americans and their gang of lieutenant nations in NATO have commenced the biggest military exercises in 25 years to take place in Europe. The code name for this operation is Defender-Europe 20 but we can interpret that as Attack-Russia 20; in effect a preparation for an attack on Russia comparable to the Nazi invasion in 1941.

Other NEO articles by Black include:

- Cuban Resistance: An Example for the World[40];
- Paris and Volnovakha: The Brutal Face of Nato Terrorism[41];
- America Aggression: A Threat To The World[42];
- The Skripal Incident-Another Anti-Russian Provocation[43]; and
- War Against Venezuela Is War Against Us All.[44]

Another author, Peter Koenig, is a Swiss contributor who has written 52 articles for NEO in the last two years.[45] On his website, he says that he "writes regularly for *Global Research*; ICH [Information Clearing House]; *RT; Sputnik; PressTV; The 21st Century; TeleSUR; The Saker Blog*, NEO; and other internet sites."

In a 28 February NEO article, Koenig advanced conspiracy theories about COVID-19:

> With high probability the virus was man-made in one or several bio-warfare laboratories of which the Pentagon and CIA have about 400 around the world .... But such high-security bio-labs also exist in Canada, the UK, Israel, and Japan. Western media also are silent about the fact that the virus is directed specifically at the Chinese race, meaning, it targets specifically Chinese DNA.

> Almost all the deaths or infected people in the 33 countries and territories to which the virus spread, are of Chinese origin. ... this is in whatever way you want to turn it, a bio-war against China.[46]

Australian NEO contributor James O'Neill has written 123 articles since 2015.[47] Five of his first 15 articles were on the topic of the downing of Malaysian Airlines Flight 17 in 2014. In these articles, O'Neill consistently gives credence to Russian denials of involvement while finding fault with the Dutch-led investigation.

O'Neill also writes for the *American Herald Tribune*, a website that Facebook and Google officials have said is linked to Iranian state media, according to a CNN article.[48] It disingenuously describes itself as "genuinely independent online media outlet." *American Herald Tribune* also lists as authors Peter Koenig and other contributors at NEO, as well as and several contributors from the Russian-state-linked Strategic Culture Foundation (SCF), including Finian Cunningham, Frederico Pieraccini, and Pepe Escobar.[49]

Another frequent NEO author was until recently a member of the tiny, hardline communist Workers World Party (WWP). The WWP was "created by the KGB," according to Lieutenant General Ion Mihai Pacepa, the former acting head of Romania's foreign intelligence service in the 1970s.[50] Pacepa, who defected to the United States in 1978, writes:

> The WWP was created by the Soviet KGB in 1957, with the initial task of helping the Kremlin create a favorable impression of the 1956 Soviet invasion of Hungary among the trade unions and "colored" population of the United States. It was run by a Soviet-style secretariat whose members were secretly indoctrinated and trained by the KGB, which also financed its day-to-day operation.[51]

The WWP now supports the regimes in China, North Korea, Cuba, and Russia.[52]

Reprints of NEO Articles

In addition to the *American Herald Tribune*, NEO articles and authors appear in other publications, including:

- *Qoshe*, an online publication that says it seeks to provide "diverse points of view and opinions" from dozens of worldwide publications.[53] Many are respectable publications but *RT, Sputnik, TASS, PressTV*, and *China Daily* are also included, along with NEO authors such as Viktor Mikhin.[54]

- Vijayvaani.com, an Indian English-language website that describes itself as "[t]he complete opinions forum."[55] It includes articles by:

  - James O'Neill, an author at NEO since 2015, debuting on Vijayvaani.com on 18 May 2020 with the article, "Devastating Revelations About the Truth Behind the Destruction of MH17," reprinted from NEO.[56]
  - Viktor Mikhin, including his February 28 2020 NEO article "US Wages Biological Warfare against China."[57]
  - Pepe Escobar, who writes for SCF.[58]
  - Israel Shamir, "a Swedish writer and journalist, known for promoting antisemitism and Holocaust denial."[59]

- *New Age*, which describes itself as "The Outspoken Daily", is published in Bangladesh. It has published NEO articles by Yuriy Zinin, Vladimir Terehov, Viktor Mikhin, and others.[60]

- *The Fringe News*, which bills itself as "Alternative News Gone Mainstream," republishes many NEO articles.[61] The site contains no information about who runs it. The "About Us" section is completely blank. There is also no contact information.[62]

- CounterCurrents.org, a website in India founded in 2002.[63]

- *OffGuardian*, which reprints many articles from NEO authors, including 49 by [Christopher Black](#) or mentioning him, and [James O'Neill](#).[64] The publication takes its name from the fact that "its founders had all been censored on and/or banned from the Guardian's 'Comment is Free' sections."

- [Veterans Today](#), whose managing editor said NEO has been a "wonderful partner" and described their cooperation as "a marriage made in heaven."[65]

New Eastern Outlook's Social Media Platforms as of June 2020

The BBC [reported](#) in July 2019 that NEO's "Facebook and Twitter accounts have been suspended."[66] NEO's other social media platforms are as follows:

Platform	Language	Engagement
Facebook	[English](#)	[19,432 likes](#), account suspended.
YouTube	[English](#)	3,150 subscribers; 390,457 total views
GAB	[English](#)	45 followers
Pinterest	[English](#)	31 followers
VKontakte	[English](#)	575 followers

Proxy Site Profiles

Global Research

COVID-19: Further Evidence that the Virus Originated in the US

By Larry Romanoff
Global Research, March 11, 2020

Region: USA
Theme: Intelligence, Science and Medicine

It would be useful to read this prior article for background:

China's Coronavirus: A Shocking Update. Did The Virus Originate in the US?

By Larry Romanoff, March 04, 2020

Global Research *article falsely blaming the United States for creating COVID-19.*

Summary

Global Research is a home-grown Canadian website that has become deeply enmeshed in Russia's broader disinformation and propaganda ecosystem. Its large roster of fringe authors and conspiracy theorists serves as a talent pool for the Russian and Chinese websites with which *Global Research* has partnered since the early 2010s. Its publications also provide a Western voice that other elements of the ecosystem can leverage to their advantage.

Introduction

Global Research is the name of the website of the Centre for Research on Globalization in Canada.[67] It launched in August 2001 and has been a steady source of anti-U.S. and anti-Western disinformation and propaganda ever since. *The Economist* referred to it as "a hub for conspiracy theories and fake stories."[68] Internet watchdog NewsGuard noted, "[t]his website severely violates basic standards of credibility and transparency."[69]

A 2006 article in the Western Standard titled "Canada's Nuttiest Professors" highlighted *Global Research*'s head Michel Chossudovsky:

> Chossudovsky has manufactured a long list of eyebrow-raising accusations that often read more like wild-eyed conspiracy theories than serious political discourse: the U.S. had foreknowledge of the 9/11 attacks ...; "Washington's New World Order weapons have the ability to trigger climate change"; the U.S. knew in advance about the December 2004 Indian Ocean tsunami, but kept it to themselves (apparently so they could ride to the rescue of devastated coastal regions); big banking orchestrates the collapse of national economies.[70]

As an example of *Global Research*'s work, its 9/11 Reader, edited by Chossudovsky, relies heavily on 9/11 "truther" claims, including those of French conspiracy theorist Thierry Meyssan.[71] The French newspaper *Liberation* called Meyssan's 2002 book 9/11: The Big Lie "a tissue of wild and irresponsible allegations, entirely without foundation."[72]

Although the content featured on the site is fringe, *Global Research* has substantial reach. A 2017 article in Canada's *The Globe and Mail* noted:

> The site has posted more than 40,000 of its own pieces since it was launched in 2001, according to one long-time contributor. But it does more: It picks up reports from other, often obscure websites, thus giving them a *Global Research* link. Those reports often get cross-posted on a series of other sites or aggressively spread across Facebook and Twitter by followers who actively share or retweet them, including a number of social botnets, or bots – automated accounts programmed to spread certain globalresearch.ca content.[73]

Michel Chossudovsky

Global Research founder and head Michel Chossudovsky is a retired professor who runs the website from his "upscale condo in Old Montreal."[74] Chossudovsky has backed and embraced anti-Western world leaders. In 2004, he volunteered to serve as a witness for former Yugoslav president Slobodan Milosevic at his trial for war crimes including genocide and crimes against humanity.[75] In 2011, he and the *Global Research* team extended warm birthday greetings to "Comandante Fidel" Castro of Cuba, saying, "You are the source of tremendous inspiration." After Chossudovsky met Castro in 2010, he said:

> I discovered a man of tremendous integrity, with an acute mind and sense of humor, committed in the minute detail of his speech to social progress and the advancement of humankind ....

> On a daily basis, Fidel spends several hours reading a large number of detailed international press reports (As he mentioned to me with a smile, "I frequently consult articles from the *Global Research* website" ...)[76]

Chossudovsky used to be a regular contributor to the Russian state-funded outlet *RT*, and *Global Research* often republishes *RT*'s content.

Collaboration with *Strategic Culture Foundation, The 4th Media*, and *SouthFront*

Global Research is deeply entwined with other outlets in Russia's disinformation and propaganda ecosystem. As described in the included profile on the *Strategic Culture Foundation* (SCF), *Global Research* has been a partner of SCF since 2011, and with the Chinese website *The 4th Media*, and its successor *The 21st Century* since 2012. In 2012, not long after *The 4th Media* had been formed, Chossudovsky was named as a member of its international advisory board, becoming its chair in 2015.[77]

Global Research has served as an author talent pool for SCF, *The 4th Media*, and *The 21st Century*. In its first ten years of operation from 2001 to 2011, *Global Research* built a large cadre of authors. Some authors who started off writing for *Global Research* later moved to partner sites. For example, Finian Cunningham wrote 187 articles for *Global Research* from 6 January 2010 to 26 September 2012, close to six articles per month, when he suddenly stopped.[78] Six weeks later, his first article for SCF was published, and he resumed this pace of production writing more than 550 articles through May 2020.[79] Similarly, Pepe Escobar began writing articles for *Global Research* in 2005 and ten years later became an SCF author.[80]

In addition, *Global Research* also republishes stories from its partner sites. For example, Federico Pieraccini became an SCF author on 23 July 2016.[81] On the same day, his initial SCF article was republished by *Global Research*.[82] About 100 of his SCF articles have since been republished by *Global Research*.[83] In 2016 and 2017, these articles were identified as originating on SCF.[84] Beginning in January 2018, however, his *Global Research* articles were no longer identified as being republished from SCF.[85]

Pieraccini's SCF articles have also appeared on other proxy websites examined in this report, including *SouthFront* and *Geopolitica.ru*, as well in the Russian state-funded outlet *Sputnik*.[86] He has also written for *Global Times*, which is associated with the Chinese Communist Party's *People's Daily* newspaper.[87]

Global Research frequently publishes articles from other websites in Russia's disinformation and propaganda ecosystem as well. It has published more than 1,200 articles from *SouthFront*, beginning in April 2015 when *SouthFront* was officially formed. In May 2015, *SouthFront* began to list *Global Research* as one of its partners.[88]

Linkages Among Websites Obscured in 2018

As described in the SCF profile, after 17 February 2018, *Global Research* no longer listed SCF as a partner on its website. At exactly the same time, *The 21st Century*, which revealed no information about its origins, became *Global Research*'s partner, replacing *The 4th Media*, an anti-western blog with alleged links to China. As discussed in the SCF profile, *The 21st Century* is a continuation of *The 4th Media*.

This may have been a collaborative effort by members of the network to obscure their mutual ties. From September 2010 through 8 March 2018, SCF listed *Global Research* and *The 4th Media* as partners or featured them prominently at the bottom of its homepage.[89] On 14 March 2018, no websites were listed.[90]

Similarly, on 5 August 2011 and on 4 March 2019, *The 4th Media* listed *Global Research* and SCF as preferred websites on its homepage. However, *The 21st Century*, successor to *The 4th Media*, did not link to other websites. Nevertheless, *Global Research* continued to list *The 21st Century* as a partner, indicating they maintained ties. Similarly, as discussed above, in January 2018 *Global Research* began to omit the fact that its articles by Federico Pieraccini originated from SCF, although they had acknowledged this before.

As noted in the profile of SCF, the reason for the apparently collaborative move to obscure the mutual ties within the network is unclear. However, two media articles looking into the links among the websites in November 2017 may have played a role.

In November 2017, Canada's *The Globe and Mail* asked *Global Research* head Michel Chossudovsky about its ties with Russia and Syria. They reported:

> Mr. Chossudovsky didn't want to discuss that. He ... declined to speak about how globalresearch.ca functions and whether it is aligned with Moscow or any other government.[91]

After the newspaper questioned Chossudovsky further:

> Mr. Chossudovsky responded through a lawyer, Daniel Lévesque. In a letter, Mr. Lévesque said the Centre for Research on Globalization denies that it is part of a network of pro-Russia or pro-Assad sites or that it is "affiliated with governmental organizations or benefits from their support."

Just eight days after *The Globe and Mail* article was published, the Atlantic Council's Digital Forensic Research Lab (DFRLab) ran an article on *The 4th Media*, noting its ties with SCF and *Global Research*. It stated:

> [The] 4th Media is advertised on the website of a Moscow-based Strategic Culture Foundation (SCF) …. The advertisement features the logo of The 4th Media at the bottom of the site, along with the logo of GlobalResearch.ca, a media outlet which @DFRLab repeatedly reported on and remains involved in spreading pro-Kremlin disinformation.

> Similarly, at the bottom of The 4th Media website, several logos are featured including state-sponsored media outlets, whose messaging routinely matches that of the governments which fund them, as well as the Moscow-based SCF.

> … there is no publicly available information about the relationship between The 4th Media and SCF. However, The 4th Media reposts a significant amount of content verbatim from SCF.[92]

Disinformation on COVID-19

Global Research attracted widespread attention on 12 March 2020 when in two tweets, Chinese Ministry of Foreign Affairs spokesman Zhao Lijian linked to two articles (now removed) which falsely blamed the United States for the COVID-19 outbreak.[93] Given *Global Research*'s longstanding, openly proclaimed partnership with Chinese websites, it is perhaps no accident that two of their articles were selected by the Foreign Ministry spokesperson.

The author of the two articles, Lawrence Devlin (Larry) Romanoff, identified as a Canadian writer, has pushed false narratives about alleged U.S. bioweapons previously, along with strongly anti-Western views.[94] In his *Global Research* article "Understanding China" he claimed, "Westerners live in an illusionary black and white world framed for them by the programming from their Zionist media."[95] He includes Japan as part of what he calls the "Zionist West." Romanoff lives in Shanghai and says he is "writing a series of ten books generally related to China and the West."[96]

Global Research reacted to the appearance of COVID-19 by seeking to frame it as a Western conspiracy. Between 1 March and 10 April 2020, the most popular Global Research articles posted on their Twitter account, @CRG_CRM, speculated that the virus originated in the United States and that COVID-19 was engineered by the global elite to take control of the world.[97]

Chossudovsky has also written many articles on COVID-19. One of them is "COVID-19 Coronavirus: A Fake Pandemic? Who's Behind It? Global Economic, Social and Geopolitical Destabilization," published on the Global Research site on 1 March 2020.[98] This article was republished or linked to by at least 70 different websites and publications, including:

- Econews Portal[99]
- Jamaica Peace Council[100]
- Tlaxcala[101]
- The Real Truth Blog[102]
- Australian National Review[103]
- *SouthFront*[104]

GRU Authors

Global Research published or republished seven authors attributed by Facebook to be false online personas created by The Main Directorate of the General Staff of the Armed Forces of the Russian Federation, popularly known as the GRU. Sophie Mangal, Anna Jaunger, Milko Pejovic, Adomas Abromaitis, Mariam al-Hijab, Said al-Khalaki and Mehmet Ersoy were identified by Facebook as false online personas created by the GRU, as noted in Potemkin Pages & Personas: Assessing GRU Online Operations, 2014-2019 by Renee DiResta and Shelby Grossman, published by the Stanford Internet Observatory in November 2019.[105] Altogether, these seven GRU personas are responsible for 108 articles that appear on Global Research's website.

Global Research's Social Media Platforms as of June 2020

Platform	Language	Engagement
Facebook	English	279,291 followers
Twitter	English	37,300 followers
YouTube	English	35,800 subscribers, 4,683,769 views

Proxy Site Profiles

News Front

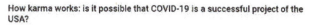

How karma works: is it possible that COVID-19 is a successful project of the USA?

30.03.2020 19:27   Share

According to the WHO report on the spread of the new coronavirus pneumonia, as of March 30, 2020, 717 992 infection cases were confirmed worldwide, 150 914 patients recovered, 33 883 cases were fatal.

Screenshot of a News Front *article falsely claiming that the U.S. could have created COVID-19.*

Summary

News Front is a Crimea-based disinformation and propaganda outlet with the self-proclaimed goal of providing an "alternative source of information" for Western audiences, a branding technique common among actors in Russia's disinformation and propaganda ecosystem. With reported ties to the Russian security services and Kremlin funding, it is particularly focused on supporting Russian proxies in Ukraine. *News Front* is one of the most blatant Russian disinformation sites, and its manipulative tactics to boost reach led to a near total dismantling of its presence on social media in early 2020.

Introduction – On the Information Front Against Ukraine

The Crimea-based *News Front* information agency was registered with Roskomnadzor, the Russian state agency that oversees mass media, in June 2015.[106] *News Front*'s parent company is Media Group News Front, co-founded by Konstantin Knyrik, the head of *News Front*.[107] According to Knyrik, *News Front* was originally called *Crimean Front*, and was established to provide informational support for Russia's attempted annexation of the Ukrainian peninsula.[108] Following the events of 2014, *Crimean Front* became *South-Eastern Front* and eventually evolved into *News Front*.

News Front operates a multi-lingual website, publishing content in Slovak, Georgian, Hungarian, French, Serbian, Spanish, German, Bulgarian, English, and Russian and claiming to have editorial branches in Bulgaria, Serbia, Germany, France, the UK, Georgia, and Hungary.[109] According to a 2018 article in *Coda*, *News Front* had ten employees and at least 100 contributors around the world.[110]

News Front's sources of funding remain opaque. Knyrik claimed that his organization was financed solely through "donations from his family, friends and income from other business activities," but a former *News Front* staffer told German publication *Zeit* that Russian security services allocate funding that makes up "a large part of the budget."[111] The Russian independent media outlet *Znak* reported that in 2016, Global Information Technologies, a civil society group founded by Knyrik and *News Front*'s chief anchor Sergey Veselovskiy, received a 3 million ruble (approximately $43,070) Presidential Grant to finance *News Front*.[112] Media Group News Front and Global Information Technologies are registered at the same address.

Time magazine questioned Knyrik's self-proclaimed independence from "government influence," pointing out that *News Front* reporters have "been granted extraordinary access" to the Russian military and are often embedded "with Russian troops and paramilitaries fighting in Syria and eastern Ukraine."[113] According to documents from Crimea occupation authority-owned V.I. Vernadsky Crimean Federal University, Media Group News Front is on its list of potential employee options for students graduating in computer science.[114]

Disinformation and Social Media Manipulation

News Front purports to provide "objective coverage," while Knyrik views the outlet as a "volunteer participant" in the information war against the West, claiming that *News Front* serves as "an alternative source of information for people in Europe and the U.S."[115] Various media outlets, however, have described *News Front* as leading "the most aggressive information war against Ukraine," following a "staunchly pro-Kremlin line;" "rarely even" pretending to "uphold traditional journalistic standards;" and inventing most of its content.[116] The Atlantic Council's DFRLab noted *News Front*'s use of photoshopped content.[117] A former *News Front* employee told *Zeit* that "certain topics...[for *News Front*'s content are] assigned directly from the [Russian] presidential administration."[118]

The EU's counter-disinformation product EUvsDisinfo has documented numerous examples of disinformation and propaganda published on *News Front*'s multi-lingual website.[119] Recent false narratives include:

- The United States created the coronavirus as a bioweapon, tested deadly viruses on humans in Ukraine and China, developed bacteriological weapons specifically aimed at certain ethnic groups, intentionally infected U.S.-based migrants with COVID-19, and transported the virus to China.[120]

- Cooperation with Europe is a catastrophe for Ukraine. Ukraine has become a colony of the IMF and George Soros and its president is a CIA puppet. Ukraine cannot control the coronavirus, as more than 1,500 Ukrainian soldiers in Donbas are infected with COVID-19. Nazis are patrolling Kyiv's streets, and a Ukrainian army veteran drove a truck into demonstrators in Minneapolis.[121]

- The EU is dead, it cannot handle the COVID-19 pandemic, and has abandoned Ukraine. The EU is inflaming the war in Donbas and is attempting to destabilize Belarus.[122]

- NATO did not provide any COVID-19 assistance to Spain, does not care about Montenegro, and spreads the coronavirus in the EU.[123]

- Bill Gates is linked to the COVID-19 outbreak and uses the pandemic to implant microchips "in whole of humanity [sic]." COVID-19 vaccines are a fraud spearheaded by Gates and Big Pharma.[124]

A screenshot of a post from the suspended News Front's *Facebook page.*

In April 2020, Facebook removed a network of accounts, including accounts associated with *News Front*, for "violating... [Facebook's] policy against foreign interference which is coordinated inauthentic behavior on behalf of a foreign entity."[125] The network posted content in Russian, English, German, Spanish, French, Hungarian, Serbian, Georgian, Indonesian, and Farsi on "topics such as the military conflict in Ukraine, the Syrian civil war, the annexation of Crimea, NATO, US elections, and more recently the coronavirus pandemic." Facebook stated that "the individuals behind this activity relied on a combination of authentic, duplicate and fake accounts...posing as independent news entities in the regions they targeted."[126] In addition to *News Front*, Facebook linked the network's "coordinated inauthentic behavior" to another Kremlin-aligned disinformation outlet, *SouthFront*, which according to Facebook is also based in Crimea.[127] (For more information on *SouthFront* and its connections to *News Front*, see the *SouthFront* profile in this report).

News Front's YouTube Takedown Elicits Response from Russian MFA

On 20 May 2020, Knyrik announced on his Facebook page that *News Front*'s channels had been removed from YouTube.[128] As of 7 April, *News Front*'s YouTube channels collectively had more than 484,000 subscribers and 479,591,989 total views. According to YouTube, the channels were "terminated for a violation of YouTube's Terms of Service."[129] Following the termination, the Russian Ministry of Foreign Affairs

(MFA) issued a statement condemning YouTube's decision.[130] Twitter also suspended *News Front*'s accounts for violating "the Twitter Rules."[131]

DFRLab, which analyzed Facebook's takedown of pages and accounts affiliated with *News Front*, found that the agency's Spanish-language pages heavily amplified content from Russian state-controlled media outlets *RT, Sputnik, TASS*, and *RIA Novosti*. According to DFRLab, the fourth-most amplified source on *News Front*'s Spanish-language web page between December 2019 and April 2020 was the Kremlin-aligned disinformation outlet *SouthFront*.[132]

The International Society for Fair Elections and Democracy (ISFED), a Georgian civil society group, concluded that *News Front*'s Facebook activity in the country included theft of platform users' identities. It detailed *News Front*'s efforts "instigating antagonism and aggression among Georgian Facebook users, dividing the society...creating political polarization" and "employing a range of tactics to spread anti-Western, pro-Russian messages."[133]

News Front Leadership: Ties to Russia-Backed Proxies in Ukraine and Russian Ultra-Nationalists

News Front previously stated that Knyrik was directly involved in the Russian operation to seize Crimea in violation of international law, including the organization of the illegitimate 2014 referendum. For his actions, he was reportedly awarded a medal from the Russian Ministry of Defense.[134] The security services of the self-proclaimed Russia-backed "Luhansk People's Republic" (LPR) awarded Knyrik a medal for cooperation.[135] In a video published in 2014, *News Front* anchor Veselovskiy claimed that Knyrik was fighting on the front lines in the so-called LPR.[136] Knyrik is reportedly banned from entering Germany for "working for the Russia-supported rebels in eastern Ukraine."[137]

Konstantin Knyrik leads the takeover of the Crimean Center for Investigative Reporting.

In March 2014, Knyrik reportedly led a raid of Russia's proxy fighters in Crimea to take over the office of the "the region's leading independent news source, the Crimean Center For Investigative Reporting," declaring that the building will now serve as the new headquarters of *Crimean Front*.[138]

Anton Shekhovtsov, a scholar of Russian and European far-right movements, documented Knyrik's ties to Russian philosopher and ultra-nationalist Alexander Dugin and the Eurasian Youth Union, both sanctioned by the United States for "actively" recruiting "individuals with military and combat experience to fight on behalf of the self-proclaimed [Donetsk People's Republic] DPR."[139] (For more information on Dugin see the *Geopolitica.ru* and *Katehon* profiles in this report). In a 2014 interview, Dugin said he had known Knyrik for more than ten years, describing him as a hero, the "vanguard of the Russian spring in Crimea," and an advocate for the inclusion of Ukraine into the "united Russian world."[140] Knyrik stated that his priority was to "focus on the creation of the empire; the first goal is to break Crimea away from Ukraine. To join it to the empire first."[141]

Knyrik and other *News Front* leaders, including its General Director Yuriy Fedin and chief anchor Sergei Veselovsky, are affiliated with the Russian ultra-nationalist Rodina party, founded by the U.S.-sanctioned Russian politician Dmitriy Rogozin.[142] Knyrik is the Committee Chairman of Rodina's regional branch. Sergei Veselovsky is the branch's Deputy Chairman. Yuriy Fedin ran on behalf of Rodina in local elections. Knyrik's page on the Russian social media platform VKontakte features many photographs of Knyrik and another U.S.-sanctioned Russian politician connected to Rodina, Sergey Glazyev, former advisor to President Putin[143] (For more information on Glazyev, see the Katehon profiles in this report.) *News Front*'s co-founder Mikhail Sinelin is Glazyev's brother-in-law, according to the Russian business daily *Kommersant*.[144] RFE/RL reported that Sinelin was a former deputy chairman of the Russian state-owned bank Vnesheconombank, and worked for about ten years in the secretariats of the Russian vice prime minister and prime minister.[145]

News Front's Social Media Platforms as of June 2020:

Platform	Language	Engagement
VK	English	1,140 members
	French	1,248 followers
	Bulgarian	1,200 members
	Russian	149,089 members
	German	1,739 members
	Serbian	1,091 members
	Spanish	1,619 members
Facebook	Russian	111 members
	French	621 followers
	French	516 followers
	English	Account suspended
	Georgian	Account suspended
	Spanish	Account suspended
	German	Account suspended
	Bulgarian	Account suspended
	Serbian	Account suspended
Twitter	English	
	Bulgarian	
	Russian	All accounts suspended
	German	
	Serbian	
	Spanish	
YouTube	English	Account suspended
	Russian	7.74K subscribers, last updated 3 years
	Russian	1.63K subscribers, last updated 4 years ago
	German	Account suspended
	International	Account suspended
	Bulgarian	Account suspended
	Serbian	Account suspended
	Spanish	Account suspended
Odnoklassniki	Russian	14,282 members
Telegram	Russian	9,995 members

Proxy Site Profiles

SouthFront

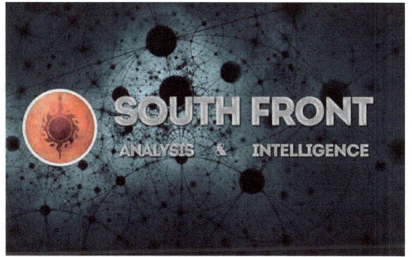

Screenshot of the SouthFront *logo.*

Summary

SouthFront: Analysis and Intelligence (a.k.a. *SouthFront*), is a multilingual online disinformation site registered in Russia that focuses on military and security issues. With flashy infographics, maps, and videos, *SouthFront* combines Kremlin talking points with detailed knowledge of military systems and ongoing conflicts. It attempts to appeal to military enthusiasts, veterans, and conspiracy theorists, all while going to great lengths to hide its connections to Russia. Evidence indicates that *SouthFront* has connections to *News Front*, another disinformation and propaganda outlet detailed in this report.

Introduction - Origins

SouthFront: Analysis and Intelligence was first registered as a formal organization to the domain registration site Reg.ru on 30 April 2015 in Moscow.[146] Currently, *SouthFront* is hosted in Amsterdam by KoDDoS, a Hong Kong-based offshore website hosting and anti-DDoS company.[147] Its content is currently available in English, Russian, and German, with the website previously featuring content in Arabic, Czech, French, and Farsi at various periods in its history.

Facebook accounts associated with *SouthFront* were [removed](#) by the platform in April 2020 for "violating… [Facebook's] policy against foreign interference which is coordinated inauthentic behavior on behalf of a foreign entity."[148] The network posted content on "topics such as the military conflict in Ukraine, the Syrian civil war, the annexation of Crimea, NATO, US elections, and more recently the coronavirus pandemic" in Russian, English, German, Spanish, French, Hungarian, Serbian, Georgian, Indonesian, and Farsi. Facebook [stated](#) that "the individuals behind this activity relied on a combination of authentic, duplicate and fake accounts…posing as independent news entities in the regions they targeted."[149]

In addition to *SouthFront*, which Facebook claimed was based in Crimea, the company linked the network's "coordinated inauthentic behavior" to *News Front*, another Kremlin-aligned Crimea-based disinformation outlet covered in this report. While *SouthFront* [claimed](#) that it "has no connection to *News Front* nor operations in Crimea," there are multiple indications to the contrary.[150] In fact, evidence indicates that *News Front* and *SouthFront* at least began as sister organizations.

According to *News Front*'s founder and leader Konstantin Knyrik, *News Front* was [originally](#) called *Crimean Front* and was established to provide informational support for the Russian attempted annexation of Crimea.[151] After 2014, *Crimean Front* became *South-Eastern Front* and then evolved into *News Front*. In a 2015 [online correspondence](#) with one of its initial official partners, the now defunct pro-Russian, pro-Assad disinformation outlet *Syrian Free Press*, *SouthFront* claimed that YouTube removed its channel named *Crimean Front*.[152]

South Front *said:*   April 24, 2015 at 20:10

Please help me
Our channel was illegal deleted by Youtube. Our new channel is
https://www.youtube.com/user/crimeanfront

Help disseminate our uppeal, please:

WARNING: SOUTH FRONT YOUTUBE CHANNEL WAS DELETED

Screenshot of a 2015 online correspondence between SouthFront *and* Syrian Free Press.

An archived 2014 page of the *Crimean Front* YouTube channel (Крымский Фронт) includes several [links](#) to its affiliated pages on other social media platforms, including a [page](#) on the Russian platform VKontakte titled "События. Интернет ополчение 'КРЫМ ФРОНТ'" ("Events. Internet militia 'Crimea Front'").[153] The page features several photographs of Sergei Veselovksiy, *News Front*'s current chief anchor, suggesting that he was affiliated with *Crimean Front*. An archived [page](#) from *Crimean Front*'s website showcases Veselovkiy's program and promotes a YouTube channel named Южный Фронт (Southern Front) under the headline "We are on YouTube."[154]

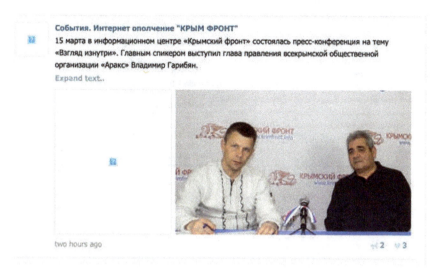

Screenshot of a post from the "Events. Internet militia 'Crimea Front'" archived VKontakte page featuring Veselovskiy (on the left).

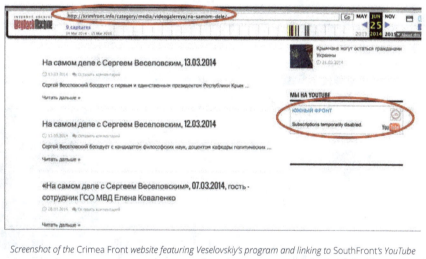

Screenshot of the Crimea Front website featuring Veselovskiy's program and linking to SouthFront's YouTube channel.

An archived 2014 VKontakte post from *Crimean Front* promoted a post from another VKontakte page titled Южный Фронт (Southern Front), announcing the creation of a new "internet-militia" called *Southern Front*.[155] According to the post, *Crimean Front*'s "principles and ideas" served as the "ideological and spiritual platform for the warriors of *Southern Front*."

События. Интернет ополчение "КРЫМ ФРОНТ"	Events. Internet militia "CRIMEA FRONT"
Присоединяйтесь - http://vk.com/ygfront	Join – http://vk.com/ygfront
☞ ЮЖНЫЙ ФРОНТ Mar 21, 2014 at 4:06 pm	**SOUTHERN FRONT** Mar 21, 2014 at 4:06 pm
Внимание! Интернет-ополчение «Южный фронт»	Attention! Internet militia "Southern Front"
В Сети сегодня заявит о себе интернет-ополчение «Южный фронт». Идея прорыва информационной блокады, запущенная крымчанами, набирает обороты. Принципы и идеалы, которые исповедует интернет-ополчение «Крымский фронт», стали надежной идеологической и духовной платформой для бойцов «Южного фронта».	The Internet militia "Southern Front" will announce itself today on the net. The idea of breaking the information blockade, launched by the Crimeans, is gaining momentum. The principles and ideals, preached by the internet-militia "Crimean Front," have become a reliable ideological and spiritual platform for warriors of the "Southern Front."

Screenshot (translated on the right) from the archived Crimean Front VKontakte page announcing the creation of the "Internet-militia 'Southern Front'".

Southern Front's archived VKontakte page titled Донецкая Республика | Русское лето! (Donetsk Republic. A Russian summer!) lists its location as Donetsk, Ukraine and links to several social media accounts, including a Twitter account still administered today by *SouthFront* (see below).[156]

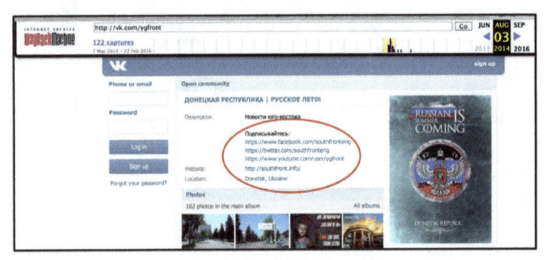

A screenshot of the archived VKontakte page.

An examination of the archived pages of the *Crimean Front* YouTube account that *SouthFront* had claimed as its own demonstrates its transformation from Крымский Фронт (*Crimean Front*) to Южный Фронт (*Southern Front*) to *SouthFront*. The names of the page change but the YouTube URL remains the same. A screenshot of the channel's 'About' page from 2016 confirms this evolution, showing the full *SouthFront: Analysis and Intelligence* name alongside the *Crimean Front* URL and a description very similar to the 'About' page on *SouthFront*'s current website.[157]

A screenshot of the archived YouTube page Крымский Фронт (Crimean Front).

A screenshot of the archived YouTube page Южный Фронт (Southern Front) showing via the circled URL that it is the same as the Крымский Фронт (Crimean Front) page.

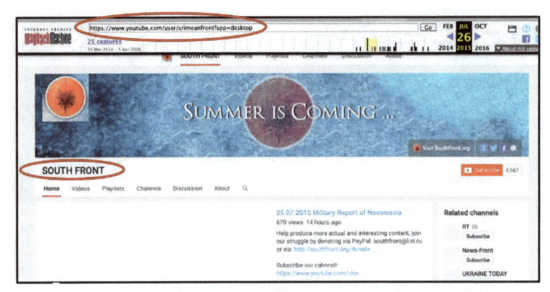

A screenshot of the archived YouTube page South Front showing via the circled URL that it is the same as the previous Крымский Фронт (Crimean Front) and Южный Фронт (Southern Front) pages.

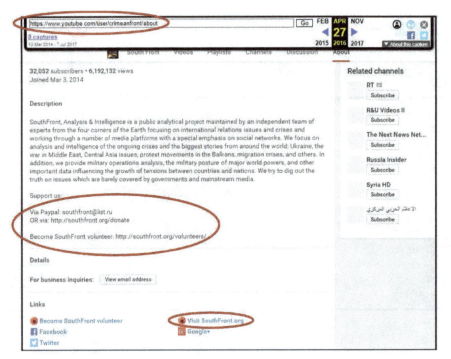

A screenshot of the channel's 'About' page showing the full SouthFront: Analysis and Intelligence *name alongside the Crimean Front URL and a description very similar to the 'About' page on* SouthFront's current website.

Denying Russian Links

Despite the evidence of its true origins and its Moscow registration, *SouthFront* goes to great lengths to appear not to be Russian. The website's About page says, "*SouthFront: Analysis & Intelligence* is a public analytical umbrella organization created and maintained by a team of experts and volunteers from the four corners of the Earth. … Everybody can become a volunteer in our organization and share their own story and perspective with the world."[158] *SouthFront*'s PayPal address has a .ru address. The anonymous submission of content and reliance on anonymous donations provide additional layers of concealment to the site's managers.[159] There is no publicly-known owner or founder of *SouthFront*, though it has previously mentioned having a "Steering Committee."[160] Per a denial issued by *SouthFront* in reaction to a Bellingcat report on the outlet, "*SouthFront*'s founder is another person and all members of *SouthFront*'s Steering Committee know very well who he is."[161]

The metadata for at least the first 20 articles published by the outlet indicate that the same user account, uchfka32, is responsible for uploading all of these initial articles as well as many of the articles published recently. In addition to user account uchfka32, four other primary accounts appear to be the most prolific content uploaders in *SouthFront*'s metadata: JJsd95, another_try, dim27348, and 9fjapsi_EE. It is difficult to attribute these user accounts to any of the *SouthFront* authors given that many articles are uploaded without authors or republished from other outlets. One possibility is that these user accounts belong to the members of the aforementioned "*SouthFront* Steering Committee," a group that is generally only mentioned in *SouthFront* articles pertaining to the 'censorship' of *SouthFront* social media properties or exposés on the outlet.[162]

One person who openly claims to be on the Steering Committee is *SouthFront* Press Officer Viktor Stoilov, a Bulgarian marketer who runs a digital advertising and strategy company based in Sofia.[163] As of early June 2020, Stoilov had authored 82 articles for *SouthFront*, with his earliest article dating back to 16 June 2015. Other authors for *SouthFront* include J. Hawk, Daniel Deiss and Edwin Watson, who are often referred to as members of the "SF Team."[164] In addition to authoring articles on their own and in different group configurations, some of these authors also serve as translators. For example, J. Hawk is commonly credited as a translator from Russian to English for *SouthFront*.

Content

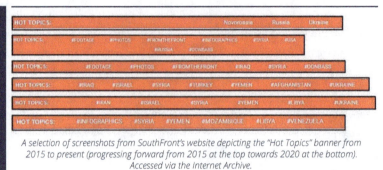

SouthFront focuses primarily on issues of military conflict, military technology, and international relations, with more specific topics typically tracking Kremlin priorities.

A selection of screenshots from SouthFront's website depicting the "Hot Topics" banner from 2015 to present (progressing forward from 2015 at the top towards 2020 at the bottom). Accessed via the Internet Archive.

The below list is a sample of *SouthFront*'s original content which directly aligns with Kremlin talking points and disinformation:

- "Distraction Tactics: Reports of Chinese and Iranian Hacking, Russians Behind Protests"[165]
- "How and Why the US Government Perpetrated the 2014 Coup in Ukraine"[166]
- "Documentary on MH17 Reveals 5-Year-Long String of Lies"[167]
- "Another Step Towards Ukraine-Like Scenario for Belarus"[168]
- "The Venezuela-Iran Axis of Unity and Resistance Stands the Test of Time"[169]
- "OPCW Manipulated Chemical Weapons Report On Syria's Douma by Removing Critical Details"[170]
- "Russia Comments on U.S. Accusations Over Aleppo Chemical Attack, Says Washington is Trying to Whitewash Actions of Terrorists"[171]

SouthFront also republishes official Russian government statements, as well as content from official Russian state media outlets, such as *TASS* and *Sputnik.*[172] By distancing itself from Russia on paper, *SouthFront* aims to build a brand that provides "alternative viewpoints" while consistently pushing pro-Kremlin disinformation and propaganda. *SouthFront* has previously responded to accusations from EUvsDisinfo alleging it is a Russian disinformation outlet by citing isolated examples of when it has been critical of the Russian government—such as criticizing the Moscow government's "draconian" response to COVID-19—as proof that it is not serving Russian interests.[173] This tactic of dispensing a drop of seemingly honest water in an ocean of Kremlin-aligned disinformation is a common practice among outlets that aim to hide their links to Russia.

COVID-19 Disinformation

SouthFront's recent content includes disinformation and dangerous claims related to COVID-19. This includes posting articles authored by Peter Koenig of *Global Research*, an example of how sites in the ecosystem leverage each other's content. *SouthFront* defends Koenig's work as the product of an individual with great professional experience, yet Koenig's writing is conspiracy-ridden and often rife with controversial rhetoric and praise for authoritarian regimes.[174]

The below examples of additional COVID-19 disinformation include both *SouthFront*-produced content and republication of disinformation from other outlets:

- "Phenomena of Coronavirus Crisis:" "Financial circles and governments are using the coronavirus to achieve own financial and political goals"[175]

- COVID-19 -- The Fight for a Cure: One Gigantic Western Pharma Rip-Off: "The real question is – are vaccines – or a vaccine – even necessary? Maybe – maybe not. The production of vaccines is pushed for profit motives and for an important political agenda for a New World Order"[176]

- The Coronavirus COVID-19 Pandemic: The Real Danger is 'Agenda ID2020:' "There is not the slightest trace of a pandemic... If indeed force-vaccination will happen, another bonanza for Big Pharma, people really don't know what type of cocktail will be put into the vaccine, maybe a slow killer, that acts-up only in a few years – or a disease that hits only the next generation – or a brain debilitating agent, or a gene that renders women infertile .... all is possible – always with the aim of full population control and population reduction."[177]

- USA Plan; Militarized Control of Population. The 'National COVID-19 Testing Action Plan:'" "The 'pandemic response body' would above all have the task of controlling the population with military-like techniques, through digital tracking and identification systems, in work and study places, in residential areas, in public places and when travelling. Systems of this type – the Rockefeller Foundation recalls – are made by Apple, Google and Facebook."[178]

- Finally! EU Blames 'Kremlin Disinformation' for Coronavirus Crisis: "EU bureaucrats and affiliated propaganda bodies are doing something that all has expected a long time ago – blaming Russia for the crisis over the outbreak of coronavirus."[179]

- COVID-19 Crisis in Russia; lockdown Craziness and Opposition Provocations: "Summing up, it becomes obvious that anti-government Western-backed forces are trying to use the COVID-19 crisis to destabilize the situation in Russia."[180]

Weak Lines of Defense

When *SouthFront* tries to refute claims it is proliferating Russian narratives, it generally falls back on two main arguments.[181] The first is that *SouthFront* is an "international team of authors and experts" with no ties to any state. This fails to explain why *SouthFront* refuses to reveal its founder(s), Steering Committee members, and main authors. The second line of defense is that *SouthFront* republishes articles from many other likeminded outlets often written by people with "advanced academic degrees." Leveraging people with "advanced academic degrees" is a common tactic used by many outlets in the Russia's disinformation and propaganda ecosystem, as detailed in this report.

Niche Graphics Capabilities

SouthFront also produces professionally designed infographics, maps, detailed "Military Situation" updates, and videos focused on troop movements, weapons systems, and conflict zones.[182] These videos can now be found on *SouthFront*'s website under the header "SF TV" and on *SouthFront*'s new YouTube channel, iterations of which have been removed by the platform in the past. Native English-speaking voiceover actors frequently narrate videos.[183]

An example of one of SouthFront's infographics depicting A Russian KH-35UE anti-ship missile

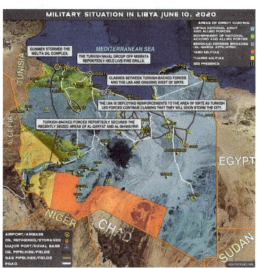

A SouthFront map depicting the military situation in Libya on June 10, 2020.

An example of one of SouthFront's video "War Reports."

Partners in the Ecosystem

From the beginning, *SouthFront* has officially partnered with other key players in the Russia's disinformation and propaganda ecosystem. As referenced in the profile on *Global Research*, *SouthFront* articles have been republished on *Global Research*'s website more than 1,200 times since mid-2015. As seen below, *SouthFront* once openly displayed its list of partners on its homepage and made frequent alterations to it. This changed sometime between 31 October 2018 and 6 November 2018 when the "Partners" column was removed from the website without explanation.

From left to right: SouthFront "Partners" columns from June 2015 to December 2015 and the last site screenshot containing the "partners" column from 30 October 2018.

In addition to its stated partnership with *Global Research*, *SouthFront* has republished content from many other disinformation outlets, including the *Strategic Culture Foundation* and *New Eastern Outlook*. In many cases, this republication of content is mutual.

Syrian Free Press - A Window into Coordination

In an unusual instance of public coordination, *SouthFront* and one of its initial named partners, the *Syrian Free Press* site visible above, agreed on the latter's "General-Contacts" page to cooperate and "better spread the real news from Ukraine and Novorossia."[184] After this initial exchange from December 2014 (pictured below), the *SouthFront* user follows up on 24 April 2015 (immediately before the official registration of *SouthFront*) to ask that *Syrian Free Press* appeal to YouTube on its behalf to restore its original "SouthFront" channel and visit its new channel, "Crimean Front" (referenced earlier for its connections to *News Front*).[185] The *Syrian Free Press* editors reply, saying "Job done. You will receive a private email from us."[186]

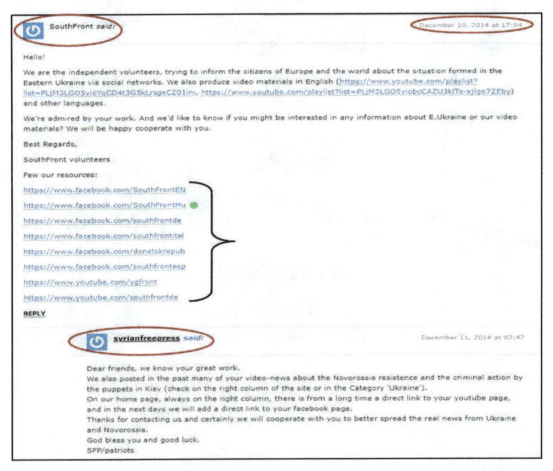

A screenshot from Syrian Free Press' *website showing an exchange between* Syrian Free Press *and* SouthFront *regarding potential cooperation.*

SouthFront's Social Media Platforms as of June 2020

Platform	Language	Engagemen
Facebook	Hungarian Multiple Accounts	11,483 followers Removed April 2020
Twitter	English German	27,500 followers 178 followers
YouTube	English English, multiple languages	Live - created 5 May 2020 - 7.08K subscribers Suspended 1 May 2020 (*SouthFront* requested that the Russian Foreign Ministry appeal on its behalf to no avail.)[187]

Proxy Site Profiles

Geopolitica.ru

Screenshot of a Geopolitica.ru article promoting conspiracy theories around Bill Gates.

Summary

Geopolitica.ru serves as a platform for Russian ultra-nationalists to spread disinformation and propaganda targeting Western and other audiences. Inspired by the Eurasianist ideology of the Russian philosopher and ultranationalist Alexander Dugin, *Geopolitica.ru* views itself as caught in a perpetual information war against the Western ideals of democracy and liberalism. The website's cooperation with other outlets in the Russia's disinformation and propaganda ecosystem broadens the reach of its messaging, which seeks to destabilize and weaken Western institutions. It publishes in English, Russian, Spanish, Italian, Serbian, French, Polish, Arabic, and Urdu.

Introduction - "Carthago Delenda Est"

Geopolitica.ru is an online portal based in Russia which serves as a megaphone for the 'Eurasianist' ideas of the prominent ultranationalist Russian philosopher Alexander Dugin.[188] Dugin's ideology is based on the belief that "there is an irresolvable confrontation between the Atlanticist world (principally the United States and the United Kingdom) and Eurasia (predominantly Russia, Central and Eastern Europe and Asia) that resists U.S.-led globalization and ethno-cultural universalization."[189] This "resistance" is reflected in *Geopolitica.ru*'s slogan "Carthago delenda est" (Carthage must be destroyed), in which liberal democracies are perceived as the "Eternal Carthage" and Russia as the "Eternal Rome."[190]

Dugin gained notoriety for propagating fascist views and was reportedly influential in Kremlin circles, until falling out of favor for criticizing Russian President Vladimir Putin.[191] According to Anton Shekhovstov, a scholar of Russian and European far right movements, Dugin was dissatisfied because Putin did not turn the 2014 attempted annexation of Crimea into a full conquest of Ukraine.[192]

To realize its vision of weakening and eventually destroying the Western liberal world order that it posits as an enemy, *Geopolitca.ru* appears to follow the principles of the "program of subversion, destabilization, and disinformation" outlined by Dugin in his 1997 book *Foundations of Geopolitics*. He advocates using the Russian intelligence services "to introduce geopolitical disorder into internal American activity, encouraging all kinds of separatism and ethnic, social and racial conflicts, actively supporting all dissident movements-extremist, racist, and sectarian groups, thus destabilizing internal political processes in the U.S."[193]

Geopolitica.ru has connections with other sites and groups that also serve as proliferators of Russian disinformation and propaganda, especially Katehon, as detailed below.[194]

The "Eurasianist" Approach to a "Multipolar World"

Established in 2008 as a Russian-language website, *Geopolitica.ru* launched an English-language page in 2012, and between 2017 and 2019 expanded to include versions in Spanish, Italian, Serbian, French, Polish, Arabic, and Urdu.[195] The portal describes itself as "a platform for...[the] monitoring of the geopolitical situation in the world" following the "Eurasian approach."[196]

Geopolitica.ru also claims to "promote a multipolar world," while rejecting liberalism, communism, and fascism. The website's proclaimed objection to fascism is disingenuous, considering Dugin's reported praise for the projects of the Nazi paramilitary organization Schutzstaffel (SS) and its pseudo-research institute, the Ahnenerb.[197] The concept of the "multipolar world" championed by *Geopolitica.ru* translates into a Dugin-envisioned world where Russia dominates its neighbors: divides Georgia; annexes Ukraine, Finland, Serbia, Romania, Bulgaria and Greece; and "gives away" Azerbaijan to Iran.[198]

In 2008, Dugin and his followers from the Eurasian Youth Union (a youth wing of Dugin's Eurasia Party) travelled to the Russian-occupied Georgian region of South Ossetia.[199]

Dugin and followers in South Ossetia in 2008

In 2015, Dugin was sanctioned by the United States along with other leaders of the Eurasian Youth Union for "actively [recruiting] individuals with military and combat experience to fight on behalf" of Russia-backed forces in Ukraine.[200]

Geopolitica.ru's Role in Russia's Disinformation and Propaganda Ecosystem

Some of the partners listed by *Geopolitica.ru* include the International Eurasian Movement (IEM), the Center for Geopolitical Expertise, the Center for Conservative Studies, and "some ex-members of the *Katehon* think tank," all of which are affiliated with Dugin.[201] *Katehon*, where Dugin used to be a member of the supervisory board, is a pseudo-think tank with apparent links to the Russian state and intelligence services (see Katehon profile in this report). *Geopolitica.ru*'s listed physical address matched the same address occupied by *Katehon* until April 2019.[202] Its chief editor, Leonid Savin, was formerly *Katehon*'s chief editor.[203] Savin is affiliated with the IEM and is reportedly a member of the Military-Scientific Society of the Russian Ministry of Defense. Dugin is also an associate of *Katehon*'s sponsor, Konstantin Malofeyev.[204] The United States sanctioned Malofeyev as "one of the main sources of financing for Russians promoting separatism in Crimea" and bankrolling "separatist activities in eastern Ukraine."[205]

Geopolitica.ru and other proxy sites that proliferate Russian disinformation and propaganda often republish each other's content. Savin, for example, is a regular contributor to the *Strategic Culture Foundation* (SCF).[206] His articles are occasionally posted on *Global Research* and *Fort Russ News*. He has also been featured on *NewsFront* and on the Russian state-funded media outlets *RT* and *Sputnik*.[207]

Geopolitica.ru reprints articles from *Fort Russ News* including an article with disinformation that the 2016 ISIS terrorist attack in Brussels was a false flag operation carried out by the United States and NATO.[208] It also publishes content from *SCF*, *Global Research*, and the *New Eastern Outlook*.[209]

Geopolitica.ru published 21 articles written by Adomas Abromaitis,[210] a false persona attributed by Facebook to Russian Military Intelligence (GRU).

A sample of recent *Geopolitica.ru* articles on COVID-19 illustrates the false claims that it attempts to spread. They demonize the United States, promote anti-vaccine messaging, sow fear, and portray Europe as if it is in a state of collapse.

- "Bill Gates, vaccinations, microchips, and patent 060606" promotes a conspiracy theory attacking Bill Gates and the Microsoft Corporation for an alleged plot to control humans by inserting microchips into their bodies. The article suggests a possible link between the Microsoft's patent number WO/2020/060606 and the "number of the beast" from the "Book of Revelation."[211]

- "Russia and the coronavirus" asserts that Western media spread disinformation about the number of COVID-19 related deaths in Russia and suggests that "one of the reasons why COVID-19 mortality rates are very low in Russia is that many Russians do not get flu vaccinations imported from the West."[212]

- "New Malthusianism and the misanthrope dynasties" falsely claims that the U.S. government and Bill Gates aim to reduce the world's population, also alleging that Gates helped create the Zika virus.[213]

- "The Coronavirus and hybrid warfare" speculates that COVID-19 is a part of a U.S. strategy "aimed at undermining the economic growth of both China and other countries" or a "plot by transnational capital against Donald Trump on the eve of the presidential election."[214]

- "Former Putin's aide: Coronavirus is the US biological weapon" quotes Sergey Glazyev, a member of *Katehon*'s supervisory board member, an associate of Dugin, and a former advisor to President Putin, as claiming that the COVID-19 virus is a U.S. biological weapon targeting "mostly people of the yellow race" and blaming Great Britain for provoking Hitler at the outbreak of World War II.[215]

- "Pandemic in the service of globalization"– blames the EU/Atlanticist/Globalist powers for intentionally inflating the threat posed by the COVID-19 pandemic to "deepen the automation of society" for the benefit of "corporate capitalism" and the "world government."[216]

- "The Italian government at the time of the coronavirus" argues that the coronavirus crisis in Italy demonstrates that "the values of the Germany-dominated EU are not the values of the Italian people, and that the EU's economic recipes have been lethal for Italy.[217]

- "Pandemic and the survival policy: the horizons of a new form of dictatorship" claims that COVID-19-related restrictive measures in Western societies amount to "total surveillance of the population" and will "gradually become permanent," spelling the "end of liberal democracies and the establishments [sic] of dictatorships throughout the world." This looming "dictatorship" is described as potentially "harsher than Nazi and Soviet concentration camps."[218]

As documented by EUvsDisinfo, a project of the European External Action Service's East StratCom Task Force, additional disinformation narratives promoted by *Geopolitca.ru* included depicting the Western world as "dominated by a handful of perverts," alleging that genocide was committed against Russians in Ukraine, portraying immigrants in Europe as rapists, and trying to discredit Western NGOs by falsely accusing them of being CIA agents.[219]

Geopolitica.ru's Social Media Platforms as of June 2020

Platform	Language	Engagement
Facebook	English	1,535 followers
	Russian	12,642 followers
	French	1,331 followers
	Spanish	1,557 followers
	Portuguese	32 followers, dormant since 2019
Instagram	Russian	55 followers
Twitter	French	247 followers, dormant since 2019
	Spanish	5000 followers
YouTube	Multilingual	2.86K subscribers 485,335 views
VKontakte	Spanish	239 subscribers

Proxy Site Profiles

Katehon

Screenshot of a Katehon article translated from Arabic.

Summary

Behind the façade of a think-tank operation, Moscow-based *Katehon* is a proliferator of virulent anti-Western disinformation and propaganda via its website, which is active in five languages. It is led by individuals with clear links to the Russian state. Within Russia's broader disinformation and propaganda ecosystem, *Katehon* plays the role of providing supposedly independent, analytical material aimed largely at European audiences, with content dedicated to "the creation and defense of a secure, democratic and just international system".

Introduction - Konstantin Malofeyev's Mouthpiece

Established in 2016, the Analytical Center *Katehon* is a subsidiary of *Tsargrad*, a company founded by Konstantin Malofeyev and affiliated with Malofeyev's pro-Kremlin Tsargrad TV, Russia's self-described "first conservative informational-analytical television channel" and the "voice of the Russian orthodox majority."[220] The website publishes in five languages: English, Spanish, French, German, and Arabic.[221] The website also used to publish in Russian but has not done so since 2017.[222]

Often referred to as the "Orthodox oligarch," Malofeyev runs one of Russia's largest private foundations, the St. Basil the Great Charitable Foundation.[223] He is also the deputy head of the World Russia People's Council, an international organization led by the Russian Patriarch Kirill.[224] Malofeyev is also the head of the "pro-Putin monarchist society" the Double-Headed Eagle; and serves on the Advisory Board of the Safe Internet League, a state-linked organization ostensibly dedicated to "fighting dangerous Web content" but accused by independent Russian media of "frequently blacklisting socio-political content."[225] The Chairman of the Safe Internet League's Advisory Board is Malofeyev's long-time associate and Putin aide Igor Shchegolev. Shchegolev is the Presidential Plenipotentiary Envoy to the Central Federal District and a member of the Security Council.[226]

According to independent Russian media outlet The Bell, Malofeyev is currently "pursuing his ambition to lead a monarchist political party and build up a conservative media empire."[227] In 2014, Malofeyev was sanctioned by the United States and the European Union for funding Russia-backed forces in Ukraine.[228] In September 2019, Malofeyev established the International Agency for Sovereign Development (IASD), described by *Tsargrad TV* as the Russian attempt to "de-colonize" Africa and push the West out of the continent.[229]

State and Intelligence Ties

While claiming to be an independent organization, *Katehon*'s leadership appears to have ties to both the Russian state and the Russian intelligence services. It is of note that the German, French and Arabic versions of *Katehon*'s website do not mention the individuals serving on its supervisory board, which in addition to Malofeyev include: [230]

- Sergey Glazyev, President Vladimir Putin's former economic advisor and currently a Minister in charge of Integration and Macroeconomics at the Eurasian Economic Commission.[231] Glazyev is under U.S. sanctions related to Russia's hostile actions in Ukraine.[232]

- Andrey Klimov, Deputy Chair of the Russian Federation Council Committee on Foreign Affairs and Head of the Council's Interim Committee for the Defense of State Sovereignty and the Prevention of Interference in the Internal Affairs of the Russian Federation.[233]

- Leonid Reshetnikov, a retired Lieutenant-General of the Russian Foreign Intelligence Service (SVR), where he led the Analysis and Information Department.[234] Until 2017, Reshetnikov was the head of the Russian Institute for Strategic Studies (RISS), a Moscow-based think-tank that used to be a part of the SVR and now conducts research for the Kremlin.[235] According to press reports, RISS research has included plans for Russian interference in the 2016 U.S. presidential elections and proposals for the Bulgarian Socialist Party to "plant fake news and promote exaggerated polling data" in advance of that country's presidential elections the same year.[236] In 2016, RISS and *Katehon* co-authored a report allegedly analyzing U.S. ideology.[237]

- Alexander Makarov, a retired Lieutenant General of the Russian Federal Security Service (FSB).[238]

Since February 2017, *Katehon* has been headed by General Director Mikhail Yakushev, a Middle East scholar and the Vice President of the *St. Basil the Great Charitable Foundation*.[239] Yakushev's career included stints at a foundation run by Vladimir Yakunin, who is a U.S.-sanctioned Russian oligarch, former KGB officer, and former director of Russian Railways.[240] Yakushev also held diplomatic posts in Israel and Tunisia, and was Chief of Staff of the Russian Federation Council's Committee for Foreign Relations.[241]

Additionally, in 2018, Yakushev founded the obscure *Center for International Strategic Initiatives*.[242] According to its English-language website, which appears to be no longer operational but still accessible through the Internet Archive, the mission of the *Center for International Strategic Initiatives* is "to promote the realization of international initiatives in the interests of the public and private sector of Russia and developing Asia and Africa."[243] The *Center* has received almost no coverage in Russian- and English-language press, but according to the a 2019 article in *Confidentiel Afrique*, its President Alexander Grachev, signed a memorandum of understanding with the President of the *Strategic Center of African Affairs*, Abdelmounem Boussafita, "for economic, social and political development between Russia and all African countries."[244] Alexander Grigoriyevich Grachev is listed as one of the *Center*'s leaders in the organization's registration documents and appears to have been Russia's former Consul General in Odessa, Ukraine and a Presidential Administration official responsible for interregional ties.[245] In 2009, the *Kyiv Post* reported that the "Ukrainian government had allegedly demanded" Grachev's expulsion.[246] According to the Ukrainian information agency *UNIAN*, Grachev was suspected of intelligence activities, including the recruitment of agents. *UNIAN* cited an article from the British Times claiming Grachev was financing pro-Russian groups in Ukraine.[247]

Conspiratorial Views of *Katehon*'s Leadership

Katehon's leaders have promoted a variety of conspiracy theories:

- Glazyev, for example, claimed that COVID-19 was a U.S.-produced biological weapon; that Ukraine's President Volodymyr Zelensky (in cooperation with the United States and Israel) planned to ethnically cleanse the Russian-speaking population of eastern Ukraine and replace it with Israeli Jews; that the United States and its European partners have been training supposed Ukrainian neo-Nazis for the past 15 years; and that "sinister forces of the 'new world order' conspired against Russia in the 1990s to bring about economic policies that amounted to 'genocide.'"[248]

- Reshetnikov's eccentric worldviews include the conviction that the United States is determined to destroy Russia and masterminded World War II through its transnational companies.[249] He also argued that the United States has created terrorist organizations and that its presidents have been selected by "secret powers."[250]

- Klimov, who has been [obsessed](#) with investigating "foreign agents," sees a foreign hand in almost every domestic Russian affair that challenges the Kremlin's line.[251] Recently, he accused U.S. diplomats, YouTube, and a Russian rapper who allegedly holds dual citizenship, of organizing protests against the Moscow Duma elections.[252] While purporting to be a champion of Russian sovereignty, Klimov headed a Cyprus-based company and ran a business with a British offshore company, according to a 2017 [article](#) from the independent Russian newspaper Novaya Gazeta.[253]

Disinformation and Conspiracy Theories Promoted on *Katehon*'s Website

Katehon is frequently cited as a source of disinformation in the [EUvsDisinfo database](#), a product of the European External Action Service's East StratCom Task Force.[254] It promotes false claims ranging from conspiracy theories attacking George Soros, the Rothschild family and the Pope, to disinformation and propaganda that seeks to undermine the EU, NATO, and trans-Atlantic solidarity. *Katehon*'s sites have also spread false allegations regarding COVID-19, including the below narratives catalogued in the EUvsDisinfo database:

- the British House of Commons considers the coronavirus a blessing;
- the coronavirus is a French-made virus transferred by the Americans;
- the coronavirus is an ethnic biological weapon;
- the coronavirus is a U.S. tool to disrupt Chinese production;
- the United States owns the coronavirus and its cure;
- the original source of the coronavirus is a U.S. military biological warfare laboratory;
- the United States created coronavirus in 2015; and
- science doubts the effectiveness of vaccines.

Katehon also promotes messages aimed at undermining European solidarity, claiming that supposedly traditional values are under attack, including:

- Europe is in danger because of Ukraine's gas;
- Italy is being punished by the European Commission for supporting traditional values;
- the EU has Nazi roots; and
- Sweden's feminist government orders not to investigate rapes to protect the immigrants that committed them.

Other disinformation that *Katehon* has promoted includes:

- Pope Francis is a servant of George Soros and the global Zionist conspiracy;
- George Soros' tentacles entangle politics and generate chaos around the world;
- the Luciferian Zionist Rothchild crime family controls the Western mainstream media;

- the Holocaust was instigated by the evil Rothschilds for creating their own nation state;
- Rasputin was killed by the Anglo-Zionist empire; and
- the fire at the Notre Dame was a satanic ritual.

Katehon published 17 articles written by Adomas Abromaitis, a false persona attributed by Facebook to Russian Military Intelligence (GRU).[255]

Katehon as a Tool in Pro-Kremlin Campaigns

Katehon appears to have been established to advance the Kremlin's influence abroad with a specific focus on gaining audiences among fringe European elements. Its website features content in Russian, English, Spanish, French, German, and Arabic.[256] When the website first appeared online in 2015, it also included Italian, Portuguese, Greek, Serbian, and Slovenian pages.[257]

According to media reports, Malofeyev has served as a proxy for Kremlin priorities in Europe, sponsoring meetings and conferences of ultra conservative parties, as well as directly funding politicians and opinion makers who criticize liberal values and support the Kremlin's policies.[258] Reportedly, Malofeyev was involved in the purported annexation of Crimea, support for the Russian military-backed separatist militancy in Donbass, election meddling in Bosnia and Herzegovina, and media acquisition in Greece, Bulgaria, and Serbia. *Katehon* promotes these same overarching goals through its disinformation and propaganda activities.[259]

Additionally, *Bellingcat* found "circumstantial evidence" that Malofeyev was involved in the failed 2016 coup in Montenegro aimed to prevent that country from joining NATO.[260] Montenegrin officials claimed that *Katehon* board member Leonid Reshetnikov also played a key role in the organization of the coup.[261] In 2019, Bulgaria banned Malofeyev and Reshetnikov from entering the country for ten years in connection with espionage and money laundering charges against Nikolai Malinov, chairman of the pro-Kremlin Bulgarian National Movement of Russophiles and a recipient of the Order of Friendship award from President Putin.[262]

A prominent Russian philosopher, ultranationalist, and the leader of the International Eurasian Movement, Alexander Dugin (see *Geopolitica.ru* case study) was a *Katehon* board member and the chief editor of *Tsargrad TV* until 2017.[263] Dugin has reportedly been one of the key drivers behind Malofeyev's strategy to establish a network of pro-Kremlin politicians among the ranks of European radicals.[264] The U.S. Department of Treasury sanctioned Dugin for "being responsible for or complicit in actions or policies that threaten the peace, security, stability, or sovereignty or territorial integrity of Ukraine."[265]

In 2014, a Russian hacking group Shaltay Boltay (also known as *Anonymous International*) published email correspondence of Georgi Gavrish, an associate of Dugin and former officer at the Russian embassy in Athens.[266] The released materials included a memorandum, allegedly penned by Dugin, mapping out the European far-right into three broad factions: the Christian right, the Neo-Nazis, and the New Right.[267] Dugin predicted that these actors would become "an essential factor...in Russian-European relations," arguing that the "extremely influential" New Right faction—consisting of parties like the French National Front, the Austrian Freedom Party, the Italian Northern League, and the Alternative for Germany—would be the most suitable partner for Russia, as it "has a sympathy for Orthodoxy, supports Russia and Putin, consistently stands on anti-American and anti Atlantist positions." Dugin also claimed that the CIA and the Mossad control the neo-Nazi movements in Europe, which are often led by Jews and homosexuals.[268]

Another insightful item from Gavrish's correspondence was a document containing a list of foreign contacts with whom Dugin supposedly discussed creating a pro-Russian "information initiative."[269] The list was composed largely of European but also South American, Middle Eastern, and Asian politicians and journalists. Christo Grozev and Anton Shekovstsov have suggested that Dugin's analysis led to the creation of *Katehon*, which began operating shortly after the memorandum was written, and features "many authors" from the foreign contacts list.[270]

Katehon's Social Media Platforms as of June 2020

Platform	Language	Engagement
Facebook	English	12,155 followers
	Spanish	page currently unavailable
	Arabic	49,863 followers
	French	page currently unavailable
	German	page currently unavailable
	Russian	775 followers, not updated since 2016
Instagram	Katehon_news	70 followers
Twitter	English	Account suspended
	Spanish	Account suspended
	French	Account suspended
	Arabic	357 followers
	German	33 followers, no new posts since 2017
	Russian	828 followers, no new posts since 2016
YouTube	English	5.93K subscribers, 1,069,466 views, most recent video uploaded 2 years ago
	Serbian	24 subscribers, most recent video uploaded 4 years ago

Digital Media Analysis

Summary:

Between February and April 2020, the seven Kremlin-aligned disinformation proxy sites and organizations profiled in this report amplified narratives critical of the United States and favorable to Russian positions, particularly in relation to the COVID-19 outbreak.

Four of the outlets—*Global Research*, *SouthFront*, *New Eastern Outlook*, and *Strategic Culture Foundation*—were observed publishing one another's content on 141 occasions, indicative of possible collaboration among them. Published content appeared in a variety of languages and was shared across multiple social media platforms.

Website Analytics

The Global Engagement Center (GEC) analyzed web traffic to seven Kremlin-aligned proxy sites and organizations and their sub-domains between 1 February and 30 April 2020.[271] The table below displays the number of page visits, the number of articles published, and the average potential readership per article for each outlet during this period. As the table shows, *Global Research*, *News Front* and *SouthFront* received the most page visits and published the most articles over the three months; however, there were vast differences in the potential sizes of their readerships.[272]

At more than 350,000 potential readers per article, no other outlet had half as much reach as *Global Research*; in fact, despite authoring the greatest number of articles, *News Front* had only 12% of the number of potential readers per article (nearly 42,000), the third lowest overall. By contrast, *Geopolitica.ru* authored the second fewest articles but had the second highest potential readership per article; at more than 145,000, it was 41% the size of *Global Research*'s potential readership.

Site	Number of Page Visits [A]	Number of Articles Published	Average Potential Readership per Article [B]	Ratio of Potential Readers/Article vs. Global Research [C]
Global Research	12,370,000	2,307	351,247	--
News Front	8,950,000	3,617	41,895	0.12
SouthFront	4,300,000	1,546	126,411	0.36
Geopolitica.ru	1,480,000	224	145,304	0.41
Strategic Culture Foundation	990,000	420	48,789	0.14
New Eastern Outlook	540,000	402	17,667	0.05
Katehon	225,000	26	17,982	0.05

[A] Page visits data was retrieved from SimilarWeb on 1 July 2020 and includes outlets' main websites and sub-domains, where available.

[B] SimilarWeb potential readership is defined as the number of people who potentially saw an article based on the number of unique visitors to the publication's website.

[C] Values in this column represent the relative rate of potential readership, controlling for number of articles published, compared to Global Research, which had 351,247 potential readers per article published between 1 February and 30 April 2020.

Amplification of Russian Narratives

During the period of analysis, the seven outlets consistently embraced positions reflective of the Russian government and state-funded media. They reposted or referenced *RT* content (92 mentions), reposted or referenced *Sputnik* content (78 mentions), and referenced Russian MFA Spokesperson Mariya Zakharova (35 times).[273] These articles included opinion pieces, long-reads, and short articles, including some with links to videos.

Senior Russian officials and pro-Russian media sought to capitalize on the fear and confusion surrounding the COVID-19 pandemic by actively promulgating conspiracy theories. For example, they promoted conspiracy theories centered around false U.S. bioweapon infrastructure. We observed five of the seven outlets promoting this narrative across 30 articles. On 20 February, *New Eastern Outlook* published an article in both Russian and English claiming that the U.S. deployed a biological weapon against China.[274]

Screenshot from a New Eastern Outlook *article.*

Then on 22 February, *News Front*'s Bulgarian language edition published an adapted version of the same article.[275] On 5 March, *RT* published an article, titled "Coronavirus May Be a Product of US Biological Attack Aimed at Iran and China, IRGC chief claims " which was re-published by *Global Research* on 6 March and then by *News Front*'s German edition on 9 March.[276] On 16 March, the narrative evolved to suggest the U.S. military had used a bioweapon in Cuba, and on 18 March, another *Global Research* article asserted that China considers the virus to be a bioweapon.[277] On 20 March, *News Front* insinuated that a U.S. lab in Georgia was involved in the creation of the coronavirus—a narrative *News Front* continued to promote throughout the period examined.[278]

Cross-Platform Content Amplification

Among the seven media outlets, four were observed frequently re-posting one another's content. Specifically, among *Global Research*, *New Eastern Outlook*, *SouthFront*, and *Strategic Culture Foundation*, 141 articles were originally posted by one outlet and later re-posted by another during the three-month period of analysis. Of particular note, *Global Research* re-posted 50 videos originally published by *SouthFront*.[279] Because of this pattern of cross-posting content, these four outlets formed an especially interconnected set of nodes within the broader network of the seven websites examined. Below is a sample of articles that were recycled from one outlet to another, which demonstrates the variety of sources that potentially collaborated, the range of topics that were covered, and the varying durations between original and republication dates:

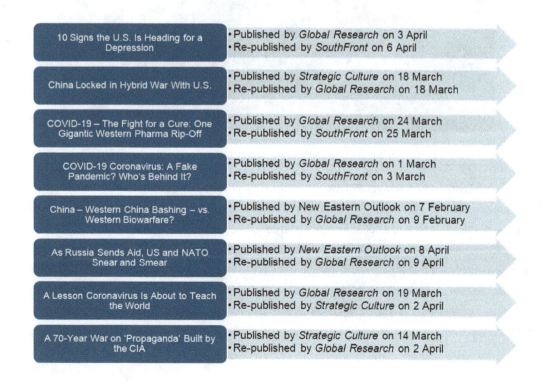

10 Signs the U.S. Is Heading for a Depression	• Published by *Global Research* on 3 April • Re-published by *SouthFront* on 6 April
China Locked in Hybrid War With U.S.	• Published by *Strategic Culture* on 18 March • Re-published by *Global Research* on 18 March
COVID-19 – The Fight for a Cure: One Gigantic Western Pharma Rip-Off	• Published by *Global Research* on 24 March • Re-published by *SouthFront* on 25 March
COVID-19 Coronavirus: A Fake Pandemic? Who's Behind It?	• Published by *Global Research* on 1 March • Re-published by *SouthFront* on 3 March
China – Western China Bashing – vs. Western Biowarfare?	• Published by New Eastern Outlook on 7 February • Re-published by *Global Research* on 9 February
As Russia Sends Aid, US and NATO Snear and Smear	• Published by *New Eastern Outlook* on 8 April • Re-published by *Global Research* on 9 April
A Lesson Coronavirus Is About to Teach the World	• Published by *Global Research* on 19 March • Re-published by *Strategic Culture* on 2 April
A 70-Year War on 'Propaganda' Built by the CIA	• Published by *Strategic Culture* on 14 March • Re-published by *Global Research* on 2 April

These four outlets often re-published their own articles in more than one language. *Global Research* posted in Italian, French, and English,[280] *New Eastern Outlook* in English and Russian,[281] *News Front* in Bulgarian and German,[282] and *SouthFront* in English and German.[283] Although these outlets tended to post one another's content, they did not tend to post translated versions of another site's content; article translations were only observed within each site.

Content Engagement by Shares on Social Media

Among the 8,542 articles published by the seven outlets between 1 February and 30 April, 1,941 (23%) were shared on Twitter via 20,670 tweets. A *Global Research* article titled "China's Coronavirus: A Shocking Update. Did the Virus Originate in the US?" posted on 4 March was among the top-five most shared articles in the data set (424 tweets). The article has since been removed by *Global Research*, but it is still referenced on the social media platform Reddit and by fringe media sites.[284] A *News Front* Spanish edition article titled "Hell in New York: One Coronavirus Death Every 17 minutes: Doctors Can't Keep Up" was shared via 388 tweets, propelling a narrative aimed at undermining public trust in the U.S. national healthcare system.[285] The most-shared Russian-language article (shared via 221 tweets) was published by *News Front*, and speculated that the EU budget under negotiation would substantially decrease support to the Baltic countries.[286]

Screenshot from a News Front Serbia *article containing the message "From Russia with Love" to underscore Russia's COVID-19 assistance to Serbia.*

In addition to Twitter, 137 articles (1.6%) were shared 15,052 times on Facebook. A *News Front* Bulgaria article praising Russia's assistance to Serbia during the coronavirus pandemic received the greatest number of Facebook shares—a total of 2,000.[287] The second-most shared article (1,381 shares) was published by *News Front Bulgaria* and reported that, according to a survey published in Foreign Affairs, residents of Crimea were confident that Russia would withstand the pressure of sanctions imposed by the United States and other Western countries.[288] The third-most shared article on Facebook was published by *SouthFront*, and reported on the killing of a senior al-Qa'ida commander in a Russian airstrike on 12 February in Western Aleppo.[289]

Twitter Analysis

Summary

The GEC analyzed Twitter mentions of seven Kremlin-aligned proxy sites and organizations: *Global Research*, *News Front*, *SouthFront*, *Strategic Culture Foundation*, *Geopolitica.ru*, *Katehon* and *New Eastern Outlook*. Twitter mentions included tweets and re-tweets that linked to articles published by these outlets, either from the outlets' Twitter accounts or from other users linking to the articles. Of these seven outlets, *Global Research* and *SouthFront* have the largest presence on Twitter, as judged by the number of Twitter accounts they operate and the number

Outlet	Mentions
Global Research	85,055
News Front	29,955
SouthFront	26,822
Strategic Culture Foundation	17,213
Geopolitica.ru	6,989
New Eastern Outlook	5,116
Katehon	2,099

of followers on each account. However, in terms of Twitter mentions, all seven outlets had their articles disseminated on the platform. Accounts tweeting these articles during the reporting period were geotagged to the UK (16%), Russia (9%), and Canada (7%). The most popular hashtags #covid19 and #coronavirus—along with a manual analysis of most-shared content, suggest that COVID-19 was the primary focus.

Report

From 1 April through 30 June 2020, the GEC identified 173,000 tweets and retweets that included links to these outlets. The table displays the number of times each outlet was linked to (mentioned) on Twitter.

Except for *Global Research* and *SouthFront*, the examined outlets have a relatively limited Twitter presence— *News Front*'s Twitter accounts have all been suspended and *New Eastern Outlook* does not have an active Twitter account. Nevertheless, content from these outlets is still shared widely on the platform. Approximately 59,000 accounts globally, excluding those in the United States, shared articles from these outlets during the reporting period. However, most of this activity came from a concentrated group of active accounts. About 1% of all the accounts in the query tweeted more than 35% of tweets sharing these articles, while the top 0.1% of accounts tweeted almost 18% of the tweets in our sample.

Account	Outlet	Followers	Last Active
@CRG_CRM	Global Research	37.4K	Present
@southfronteng	SouthFront	27.8K	Present
@GRTVnews	Global Research	19.8K	Nov 2018
@Strateg_Culture	Strategic Culture Foundation	5.6K	May 2020
@Geopoliticaesp	Geopolitica.ru	5.0K	Present
@geopolitica_FR	Geopolitica.ru	262	May 2019
@KatehonA	Katehon	368	Present

Of the 0.1% most active accounts, *News Front* was the sole outlet never tweeted by accounts tweeting articles from multiple outlets. *Global Research* and *New Eastern Outlook* were the two outlets that were most likely to be tweeted by the same account. Several of the most active accounts shared content from more than half of the outlets included in our analysis, where articles frequently spread sensationalized or questionable content, including outright disinformation. For more information regarding cross-platform content amplification among these outlets, please see the Digital Media Analysis section of this report.

According to self-reported locations, accounts tweeting these articles were concentrated in the following top ten locations:

1. UK (16%)
2. Russia (9%)
3. Canada (7%)
4. Japan (6%)
5. France (5%)
6. Spain (4%)
7. Chile (4%)
8. Venezuela (4%)
9. Germany (3%)
10. Australia (3%)

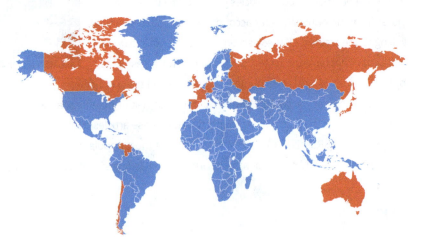

Given its prominence in the dataset, many of the overarching topics reflected the narratives promoted by *Global Research*. Across the entire dataset of tweets that amplified articles from the outlets included in this report, the most used hashtags were:

1. #covid19 (4,358 tweets)
2. #coronavirus (2,265 tweets)
3. #us (949 tweets)
4. #billgates (867 tweets)
5. #china (718 tweets)

The daily tweet volume was relatively stable across the period examined, except for a dramatic peak on 30 May. This peak was driven by extensive sharing of a *Strategic Culture Foundation* article claiming that a German official leaked a report denouncing COVID-19 as "A Global False Alarm."[290] This article, which contains misinformation downplaying the threat of COVID-19, was the most shared article—tweeted more than 15,000 times—during the reporting period. The report at the center of the article was denounced by the German government as the work of a lone employee who used the German Federal Ministry of the Interior (BMI)'s official letterhead to support the employee's private opinion.[291] The *Strategic Culture Foundation* article also references an *RT* article that includes a press release defending the BMI employee and criticizing the German Federal Ministry.[292] Although the central claims of the report have been refuted—the report was fact-checked by Health Feedback as "unsupported" and criticized by Der Spiegel for exaggerating and citing "dubious blogs"—*Strategic Culture Foundation* endorsed the false claims.[293]

Number of Tweets by Day

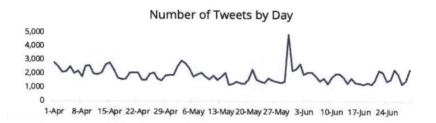

While the most widely shared article originated from the *Strategic Culture Foundation*, *Global Research* was the most prominent outlet, accounting for almost half of all the articles shared on Twitter. Most of *Global Research*'s content included sensationalized coverage or disinformation about COVID-19 and vaccines, often featuring false claims about the U.S. government or Bill Gates. Although COVID-19 disinformation was the most prominent topic, conspiracy theories were mixed in, many of them making accusations against the United States or U.S. citizens. The most widely shared articles included:

- ""Greater Israel": The Zionist Plan for the Middle East" (2,656 tweets);[294]
- "US Hospitals Getting Paid More to Label Cause of Death as 'Coronavirus'" (2,427 tweets);[295] and
- "'Mass Sterilization:' Kenyan Doctors Find Anti-fertility Agent in UN Tetanus Vaccine" (2,127 tweets).[296]

News Front was the second-most shared outlet on Twitter during the reporting period. Popular content from this outlet focused on pro-Russian narratives and geopolitics related to the United States, Eastern Europe, and Latin America. Its most popular content was written in Russian and Spanish. The most widely shared articles included:

- "Alexander Rogers: Those who betrayed their homeland lose their talent" (1,223 tweets);[297]
- "Swedish-Palestinian journalist dies just before exposing Soros and Aschberg" (873 tweets);[298] and
- "Supreme Court of Brazil asks to suspend Bolsonaro for 180 days due to its inefficiency against the coronavirus"(434 tweets).[299]

The most popular articles from *SouthFront*, the third-most shared outlet in this analysis, focused on conspiracy theories related to COVID-19, conflict in the Middle East, and criticism of the United States. Accounts sharing content from this outlet were concentrated in Japan and European nations. Most of the Japanese activity was from accounts associated with "QAnon," a conspiracy theory focused on the "deep state." The most widely shared articles included:

- "THE CORONAVIRUS COVID-19 PANDEMIC: THE REAL DANGER IS "AGENDA ID2020"" (881 tweets);[300]
- "SOUTHFRONT'S YOUTUBE CHANNEL IS BANNED" (760 tweets);[301] and
- "U.S. USED $601M SEIZED FROM VENEZUELA TO FUND BORDER WALL WITH MEXICO" (665 tweets).[302]

Strategic Culture Foundation was the fourth-most shared outlet in our analysis, with the majority of tweets linking to the article mentioned above. Other popular content from the outlet also focused on COVID-19-related disinformation that made references to the U.S. government and Bill Gates. The most widely shared articles included:

- "German Official Leaks Report Denouncing Corona as 'A Global False Alarm'" (15,020 tweets);[303]
- "Is It Time to Launch an Investigation Into the Bill & Melinda Gates Foundation for Possible 'Crimes Against Humanity?" (418 tweets);[304] and
- "What Did U.S. Intel Really Know About the 'Chinese' Virus?" (302 tweets).[305]

Geopolitica.ru, the fifth-most shared outlet, was most popular among accounts in Spanish-speaking countries including Chile, Spain, and Venezuela. Popular content from the outlet highlighted criticism of the United States, George Soros, and the modern day Western anti-fascism movement. The most widely shared articles included:

- "PUTIN: 95% OF WORLD TERRORIST ATTACKS ARE MADE BY THE CIA" (1,963 tweets);[306]
- "SOCIAL ENGINEERING: GLOBALIST SOROS WANTS ABORTIONS WORLDWIDE" (676 tweets);[307] and
- "ANTI (FASCISTS): THE GLOBALISTS' ARMY OF TERROR" (1,963 tweets).[308]

New Eastern Outlook, the sixth-most shared outlet, focused on English-language articles related to COVID-19. These articles criticized the United States and "big pharma." The most widely shared articles included:

- "Why is Trump Drumbeating a 'New Cold War' with China?" (1,078 tweets);[309]
- "The Remarkable Doctor A. Fauci" (286 tweets);[310]

Katehon was the least-shared outlet on Twitter in our analysis. Most of the accounts sharing this content were located in Europe. Many of the popular topics focused on criticizing and exposing the global "deep state." The most widely shared articles included:

- "WHO IS ENRICO SASSOON, GODFATHER OF "CASALEGGIO ASSOCIATI" AND "5 STAR MOVEMENT"?" (454 tweets);[311]
- "THE HUB OF WORLD EVIL: THE BRITISH DEEP STATE" (182 tweets); [312] and
- "EUROPE: ON THE EVE OF THE CIVIL WAR?" (43 tweets).[313]

References

[1] https://www.nytimes.com/2020/07/28/us/politics/russia-disinformation-coronavirus.html

[2] https://www.nytimes.com/2020/07/28/us/politics/russia-disinformation-coronavirus.html

[3] https://www.rusprofile.ru/id/4627728

[4] https://web.archive.org/web/20100908070545/http:/www.strategic-culture.org/

[5] https://www.nytimes.com/2020/07/28/us/politics/russia-disinformation-coronavirus.htmlhttps://www.strategic-culture.org/

[6] https://www.strategic-culture.org/

[7] http://en.interaffairs.ru/,
http://en.interaffairs.ru/partners.html

[8] https://www.rusprofile.ru/id/4627728,
https://www.latimes.com/archives/la-xpm-1989-11-22-mn-152-story.html,
https://www.washingtonpost.com/archive/politics/1990/07/15/soviets-weaken-party-politburo/e704c942-2e22-4157-8236-6c36e636897d/

[9] https://www.rusprofile.ru/founders/3857002

[10] https://xn--n1aaccga.xn--p1ai/

[11] http://www.edinaya-odessa.org/st/8850-russkoe-edinstvo.html

[12] https://web.archive.org/web/20150502152336/http:/www.strategic-culture.org/

[13] https://www.strategic-culture.org/

[14] https://www.strategic-culture.org/contributors/?letter=C

[15] https://www.strategic-culture.org/news/2013/03/10/us-psychotic-superpower-on-a-hair-trigger/

[16] https://www.strategic-culture.org/news/2013/04/20/give-north-korea-some-respect/

[17] https://www.strategic-culture.org/news/2014/04/18/putin-stands-out-as-a-real-world-leader/

[18] https://www.strategic-culture.org/news/2015/04/26/washington-choreographing-all-out-war-with-russia/

[19] https://www.strategic-culture.org/news/2015/01/03/the-year-us-led-capitalism-became-exposed-as-root-of-global-conflict/

[20] https://www.rt.com/op-ed/authors/Finian-Cunningham/,
https://sputniknews.com/search/?query=finian+cunningham,
https://ria.ru/search/?query=%D1%84%D0%B8%D0%BD%D0%BD%D0%B8%D0%B0%D0%BD+%D0%BA%D0%B0%D0%BD%D0%BD%D0%B8%D0%BD%D0%B3%D0%B5%D0%BC

[21] https://www.strategic-culture.org/contributors/?letter=C

[22] https://www.strategic-culture.org/news/2020/04/14/the-facts-about-crimea-should-be-recognised-and-so-should-crimea/,
https://www.strategic-culture.org/news/2019/11/19/washington-wants-an-arctic-circle-of-confrontation/

[23] https://www.strategic-culture.org/contributors/?letter=E

[24] https://risingtidefoundation.net/about-us/

[25] https://orientalreview.org/2019/07/16/freeland-responds-to-putin-liberalism-will-prevail-nazis-will-help/,
https://www.geopolitica.ru/en/article/londons-five-eyes-freelands-nazi-roots-stand-exposed-once-more

[26] http://canadianpatriot.org/about-us/

[27] https://risingtidefoundation.net/about-us/,
https://www.strategic-culture.org/contributors/?letter=C,
https://www.strategic-culture.org/news/2020/03/14/a-70-year-war-on-propaganda-built-by-the-cia/

[28] https://www.strategic-culture.org/contributors/?letter=K,
https://www.voltairenet.org/auteur125978.html?lang=en,
https://www.voltairenet.org/article187508.html

[29] https://www.strategic-culture.org/contributors/?letter=I

[30] https://www.strategic-culture.org/news/2015/05/01/modern-nazism-driving-force-euro-atlantic-integration/

[31] https://www.strategic-culture.org/news/2015/02/13/the-czech-republic-doomed-without-russia/

[32] https://www.strategic-culture.org/news/2014/10/05/estonia-doomed-without-russia/

[33] https://www.strategic-culture.org/news/2015/07/04/russia-has-enough-gas-for-everyone/

[34] https://www.strategic-culture.org/news/2015/07/21/brussels-kiev-duo-blackmailers/

[35] https://web.archive.org/web/20100908070545/http:/www.strategic-culture.org/,
https://web.archive.org/web/20110805041427/http:/www.strategic-culture.org/

[36] https://journal-neo.org/about/

[37] https://www.ivran.ru/en/periodicals

[38] https://journal-neo.org/

[39] https://journal-neo.org/author/christopher-black/

[40] https://journal-neo.org/2014/12/29/cuban-resistance-an-example-for-the-world/

[41] https://journal-neo.org/2015/01/22/paris-and-volnovakha-the-brutal-face-of-nato-terrorism/

[42] https://journal-neo.org/2017/04/17/america-aggression-a-threat-to-the-world/

[43] https://journal-neo.org/2018/03/09/the-skripal-incident-another-anti-russian-provocation/

[44] https://journal-neo.org/2019/03/15/war-against-venezuela-is-war-against-us-all/

[45] https://journal-neo.org/author/peterkoenig/

[46] https://journal-neo.org/2020/02/28/china-confronts-covid19-with-endless-creation-towards-a-shared-future-for-mankind/

[47] https://journal-neo.org/author/james-oneill/

[48] https://ahtribune.com/,
https://www.cnn.com/2020/01/24/tech/iran-info-ops/index.html

[49] https://www.strategic-culture.org/

[50] https://www.nationalreview.com/2003/04/still-red-ion-mihai-pacepa/,
https://www.latimes.com/archives/la-xpm-1990-01-28-mn-1248-story.html

[51] https://www.nationalreview.com/2003/04/still-red-ion-mihai-pacepa/

[52] https://www.workers.org/2019/10/43954/,
https://www.workers.org/2020/04/47443/,
https://www.workers.org/2019/01/40259/
https://www.workers.org/2018/02/35788/

[53] https://qoshe.com/who

[54] https://qoshe.com/news,
https://qoshe.com/gazete/new-eastern-outlook-en

[55] http://www.vijayvaani.com/

[56] http://www.vijayvaani.com/AuthorProfile.aspx?pid=887,

https://journal-neo.org/author/james-oneill/page/11/,

https://journal-neo.org/2020/03/27/devastating-revelations-about-the-truth-behind-the-destruction-of-mh17/

[57] http://www.vijayvaani.com/AuthorProfile.aspx?pid=738,

http://www.vijayvaani.com/ArticleDisplay.aspx?aid=5324

[58] http://www.vijayvaani.com/AuthorProfile.aspx?pid=386

[59] http://www.vijayvaani.com/AuthorProfile.aspx?pid=205,

https://www.theguardian.com/media/2011/jan/31/wikileaks-holocaust-denier-handled-moscow-cables

[60] https://www.newagebd.net/articlelist/298/Opinion,

https://www.newagebd.net/credit/Yuriy%20Zinin,

https://www.newagebd.net/credit/Vladimir%20Terehov,

https://muckrack.com/viktor-mikhin

[61] http://www.thefringenews.com/?s=new+eastern+outlook

[62] http://www.thefringenews.com/about-us/

[63] https://countercurrents.org/author/peter-koenig/

[64] https://off-guardian.org/?s=christopher+black&submit=Search,

https://off-guardian.org/tag/james-oneill/

[65] https://www.veteranstoday.com/

[66] https://monitoring.bbc.co.uk/product/c200z4k5

[67] https://www.globalresearch.ca/

[68] https://www.economist.com/united-states/2017/04/15/how-a-pair-of-self-publicists-wound-up-as-apologists-for-assad

[69] https://www.newsguardtech.com/wp-content/uploads/2020/03/GlobalResearch.ca-3-20-20.pdf

[70] http://www2.psych.utoronto.ca/users/furedy/Papers/af/wstd06.htm

[71] https://www.globalresearch.ca/the-911-reader-the-september-11-2001-terror-attacks/5303012

[72] https://www.theguardian.com/world/2002/apr/01/september11.france

[73] https://web.archive.org/web/20171117193837/https://www.theglobeandmail.com/news/world/canadian-website-in-natos-sights-for-spreading-disinformation/article37015521/

[74] https://web.archive.org/web/20171117193837/https://www.theglobeandmail.com/news/world/canadian-website-in-natos-sights-for-spreading-disinformation/article37015521/

[75] http://www.slobodan-milosevic.org/news/smorg091304.htm

[76] https://www.globalresearch.ca/happy-birthday-fidel-castro/26009

[77] https://web.archive.org/web/20121026130610/http:/www.4thmedia.org/aboutus/,

https://web.archive.org/web/20150516032538/http:/www.4thmedia.org/aboutus/

[78] https://www.globalresearch.ca/author/finian-cunningham

[79] https://www.strategic-culture.org/news/2012/11/12/high-stakes-in-bahrain-repression/,

https://www.strategic-culture.org/contributors/?letter=C

[80] https://www.globalresearch.ca/author/pepe-escobar/page/5,

https://www.strategic-culture.org/contributors/pepe-escobar/

[81] https://www.strategic-culture.org/contributors/federico-pieraccini/

[82] https://www.globalresearch.ca/failed-turkish-coup-sabotage-incompetence-or-deception/5537479

[83] https://www.globalresearch.ca/author/federico-pieraccini

[84] https://www.globalresearch.ca/middle-east-in-turmoil-trump-netanyahu-and-mohammad-bin-salman-destroyers-of-the-neoliberal-world-order/5622748

[85] https://www.globalresearch.ca/protecting-chinas-belt-and-road-initiative-from-us-led-terrorism/5625448

https://www.strategic-culture.org/news/2018/01/09/protecting-belt-road-initiative-from-us-led-terrorism-will-china-send-troops-syria/

[86] https://southfront.org/a-terrorist-attack-against-eurasian-integration/,

https://www.geopolitica.ru/es/article/los-grandes-desarrollos-sugieren-fuertemente-el-fin-del-orden-unipolar-mundial,

https://sputniknews.com/politics/201607251043602692-turkey-erdogan-military-coup/

[87] http://www.globaltimes.cn/content/1133318.shtml,

https://qz.com/745577/inside-the-global-times-chinas-hawkish-belligerent-state-tabloid/

[88] https://www.globalresearch.ca/author/southfront/page/21,

https://web.archive.org/web/20150628083839/http:/southfront.org/

[89] https://web.archive.org/web/20180308143532/https://www.strategic-culture.org/

[90] https://web.archive.org/web/20180314230228/https://www.strategic-culture.org/

[91] https://web.archive.org/web/20171117193837/https://www.theglobeandmail.com/news/world/canadian-website-in-natos-sights-for-spreading-disinformation/article37015521/

[92] https://medium.com/dfrlab/fakenews-made-in-china-576239152a84,

https://medium.com/@DFRLab

[93] https://twitter.com/zlj517/status/1238269193427906560,

https://twitter.com/zlj517/status/1238292025817968640

[94] https://www.wsj.com/articles/canadian-writer-fuels-china-u-s-tiff-over-coronaviruss-origins-11585232018

[95] https://www.globalresearch.ca/understanding-china/5695479

[96] https://www.globalresearch.ca/understanding-china/5695479

[97] https://twitter.com/crg_crm?lang=en

[98] https://www.globalresearch.ca/covid-19-coronavirus-a-fake-pandemic-whos-behind-it-global-economic-and-geopolitical-destabilization/5705063

[99] https://ecoterra.info/index.php/en/1671-covid-19-coronavirus-a-fake-pandemic

[100] https://jamaicapeacecouncil.wordpress.com/2020/03/08/covid-19-coronavirus-a-fake-pandemic-whos-behind-it-global-economic-social-and-geopolitical-destabilization-johns-hopkins-coronavirus-simulation-october-2019/

[101] http://www.tlaxcala-int.org/article.asp?reference=28245

[102] http://realtruthblog.com/current-quicklinx-3

[103] https://australiannationalreview.com/?s=chossudovsky

[104] https://southfront.org/fake-coronavirus-data-fear-campaign-spread-of-the-covid-19-infection/

[105] https://cyber.fsi.stanford.edu/io/publication/potemkin-think-tanks

[106] https://rkn.gov.ru/mass-communications/reestr/media/p67382/?id=575587&page=67382

[107] https://www.rusprofile.ru/id/7601209,

https://news-front.info/contacts/

[108] https://novorosinform.org/402691

[109] https://news-front.info/,

https://news-front.info/about/

[110] https://www.codastory.com/disinformation/armed-conflict/meet-the-kremlins-keyboard-warrior-in-crimea/

[111] https://www.codastory.com/disinformation/armed-conflict/meet-the-kremlins-keyboard-warrior-in-crimea/,

https://www.zeit.de/zustimmung?url=https%3A%2F%2Fwww.zeit.de%2Fdigital%2Finternet%2F2017-02%2Fbundestag-elections-fake-news-manipulation-russia-hacker-cyberwar%2Fkomplettansicht

[112] https://www.rusprofile.ru/founders/10433419,

https://www.znak.com/2016-07-05/kto_i_kak_poluchaet_prezidentskie_granty_dlya_nko_v_2016_godu

[113] https://time.com/4889471/germany-election-russia-fake-news-angela-merkel/

[114] https://cfuv.ru/wp-content/uploads/2016/08/090203-opop-2017-o.pdf
[115] https://news-front.info/about/,
https://news-front.info/2016/07/21/kak-dobrovolcy-nezavisimogo-agentstva-news-front-ispugali-professionalov-nemeckogo-gosudarstvennogo-telekanala-ard-konstantin-knyrik/,
https://www.codastory.com/disinformation/armed-conflict/meet-the-kremlins-keyboard-warrior-in-crimea/
[116] https://ru.krymr.com/a/27871931.html,
https://www.codastory.com/disinformation/armed-conflict/meet-the-kremlins-keyboard-warrior-in-crimea/,
https://time.com/4889471/germany-election-russia-fake-news-angela-merkel/,
https://www.zeit.de/zustimmung?url=https%3A%2F%2Fwww.zeit.de%2Fdigital%2Finternet%2F2017-02%2Fbundestag-elections-fake-news-manipulation-russia-hacker-cyberwar%2Fkomplettansicht
[117] https://medium.com/dfrlab/facebook-removes-propaganda-outlets-linked-to-russian-security-services-51fbe2f6b841
[118] https://www.zeit.de/zustimmung?url=https%3A%2F%2Fwww.zeit.de%2Fdigital%2Finternet%2F2017-02%2Fbundestag-elections-fake-news-manipulation-russia-hacker-cyberwar%2Fkomplettansicht
[119] https://euvsdisinfo.eu/disinformation-cases/?text=News+Front&date=&offset=130
[120] https://euvsdisinfo.eu/report/coronavirus-was-spread-around-the-world-from-the-worldwide-us-biological-laboratories/,
https://de.news-front.info/2020/01/25/massenepidemie-in-china-coronavirus-eine-neue-entwicklung-aus-den-biolaboren-des-pentagon/,
https://news-front.info/2020/01/30/kitajskij-koronavirus-zastavil-vspomnit-o-sobytiyah-na-ukraine-desyatiletnej-davnosti/,
https://euvsdisinfo.eu/report/us-tests-ethnic-weapons-against-slavs-in-its-biolabs-in-ukraine/,
https://en.news-front.info/2020/04/06/us-staged-coronavirus-terror-for-illegal-immigrants-migrants-plead-for-deportation/,
https://euvsdisinfo.eu/report/us-servicemen-imported-coronavirus-intentionally-into-china/
[121] https://euvsdisinfo.eu/disinformation-cases/?text=News+Front&date=&offset=110,
https://euvsdisinfo.eu/disinformation-cases/?text=News+Front&date=&offset=70,
https://euvsdisinfo.eu/report/cia-ordered-puppet-zelenskyy-extend-sanctions-against-russian-social-media/,
https://euvsdisinfo.eu/report/more-than-1500-ukrainian-soldiers-in-donbas-are-infected-with-a-coronavirus/,
https://euvsdisinfo.eu/report/kiev-stops-public-transport-nazis-are-patrolling-the-streets/,
https://euvsdisinfo.eu/report/an-ukrainian-terrorist-attack-was-perpetrated-in-the-us-a-situation-similar-to-the-2014-coup-in-kyiv/
[122] https://euvsdisinfo.eu/report/eu-is-dead-it-is-incapable-to-take-control-over-the-coronavirus-crisis/,
https://euvsdisinfo.eu/report/the-coronavirus-epidemic-proves-that-the-eu-has-abandoned-ukraine/,
https://euvsdisinfo.eu/report/kievs-western-protectors-are-inflaming-war-in-the-donbass/,
https://euvsdisinfo.eu/report/the-eu-provoked-a-civil-war-in-ukraine-now-it-destabilises-belarus/
[123] https://euvsdisinfo.eu/report/nato-did-not-help-spain-fight-coronavirus/,
https://euvsdisinfo.eu/report/nato-does-not-care-about-montenegro-amid-covid-19-pandemic/,
https://euvsdisinfo.eu/report/nato-spreads-the-coronavirus-in-the-eu/%20%20%E2%80%A2
[124] https://news-front.info/2020/03/22/v-ssha-znali-o-gryadushhej-epidemii-davno/,
https://euvsdisinfo.eu/report/bill-gates-and-other-globalists-use-the-corona-pandemic-to-implant-microchips-in-the-whole-of-humanity/,
https://euvsdisinfo.eu/report/coronavirus-vaccines-big-pharma-fraud-bill-gates/
[125] https://about.fb.com/wp-content/uploads/2020/05/April-2020-CIB-Report.pdf
[126] https://about.fb.com/wp-content/uploads/2020/05/April-2020-CIB-Report.pdf
[127] https://about.fb.com/wp-content/uploads/2020/05/April-2020-CIB-Report.pdf
[128] https://www.facebook.com/konstantin.knyrik/posts/550798279162508
[129] https://www.youtube.com/channel/UCt94dhpYv06IMOTXcGXt3eQ
[130] https://www.mid.ru/en/diverse/-/asset_publisher/zwl2FuDbhJx9/content/ob-udalenii-video-hostingom-youtube-akkauntov-telekanala-krym-24-informagentstv-anna-news-i-news-front-?_101_INSTANCE_zwl2FuDbhJx9_redirect=https%3A%2F%2Fwww.mid.ru%2Fen%2Fdiverse%3Fp_p_id%3D101_INSTANCE_zwl2FuDbhJx9%26p_p_lifecycle%3D0%26p_p_state%3Dnormal%26p_p_mode%3Dview%26p_p_col_id%3Dcolumn-1%26p_p_col_pos%3D2%26p_p_col_count%3D6
[131] https://twitter.com/News_Front_info/
[132] https://medium.com/dfrlab/facebook-removes-propaganda-outlets-linked-to-russian-security-services-51fbe2f6b841
[133] https://isfed.ge/eng/blogi/saqartveloshi-politikuri-polarizatsiis-khelshemtskobi-rusuli-sainformatsio-operatsia-feisbuqze-da-masshi-chartuli-araavtenturi-angarishebi
[134] https://news-front.info/konstantin-sergeevich-knyrik-biografiya/
[135] https://vk.com/knyrik?z=photo122769433_457248460%2Fphotos122769433
[136] https://www.youtube.com/watch?v=p0ws95DLwn8
[137] https://www.zeit.de/zustimmung?url=https%3A%2F%2Fwww.zeit.de%2Fdigital%2Finternet%2F2017-02%2Fbundestag-elections-fake-news-manipulation-russia-hacker-cyberwar%2Fkomplettansicht
[138] https://www.codastory.com/disinformation/armed-conflict/meet-the-kremlins-keyboard-warrior-in-crimea/
[139] https://anton-shekhovtsov.blogspot.com/2014/08/pro-russian-extremists-in-2006-and-2014.html,
https://www.treasury.gov/press-center/press-releases/Pages/jl9993.aspx
[140] https://www.youtube.com/watch?v=p0ws95DLwn8
[141] http://anton-shekhovtsov.blogspot.com/2016/01/how-alexander-dugins-neo-eurasianists.html
[142] https://www.rusprofile.ru/id/7601209 ,
https://en.news-front.info/contact-us/ ,
http://www.rodina.ru/novosti/V-Simferopole-proshla-konferenciya-regionalnogo-otdeleniya-vserossijskoj-politicheskoj-partii-Rodina-v-Respublike-Krym ,
https://www.themoscowtimes.com/2012/09/30/rogozins-rodina-party-reinstated-a18170,
https://www.treasury.gov/resource-center/sanctions/OFAC-Enforcement/Pages/20140317.aspx
[143] https://vk.com/knyrik?z=albums122769433 ,
https://www.treasury.gov/resource-center/sanctions/OFAC-Enforcement/Pages/20140317.aspx
https://www.bloomberg.com/news/articles/2019-08-16/putin-s-iconoclastic-economics-guru-to-lose-kremlin-post
[144] https://www.rusprofile.ru/founders/7601209,
https://www.kommersant.ru/doc/485775
[145] https://ru.krymr.com/a/27871931.html
[146] https://www.reg.ru/whois/?dname=southfront.org
[147] https://koddos.net/
[148] https://about.fb.com/wp-content/uploads/2020/05/April-2020-CIB-Report.pdf
[149] https://about.fb.com/wp-content/uploads/2020/05/April-2020-CIB-Report.pdf
[150] https://southfront.org/antiwar-about-censorship-of-southfront-on-youtube-and-facebook/
[151] https://novorosinform.org/402691
[152] https://syrianfreepress.wordpress.com/about/#comment-30479
[153] https://web.archive.org/web/20140307190510/https://www.youtube.com/user/crimeanfront,
https://web.archive.org/web/20140315135947/http://vk.com/crimeafront
[154] https://web.archive.org/web/20140625103752/http://krimfront.info/category/media/videogalereya/na-samom-dele/
[155] https://web.archive.org/web/20140322200213/http://vk.com/crimeafront
[156] https://web.archive.org/web/20140803012046/http://vk.com/ygfront,
https://twitter.com/southfronteng

[157] https://southfront.org/about-southfront/
[158] https://southfront.org/about-southfront/
[159] https://southfront.org/donate/
[160] https://southfront.org/appeal-of-southfront-steering-committee-regarding-censorship-on-youtube-and-facebook/
[161] https://maps.southfront.org/bellingcats-five-star-investigation-reveals-identity-of-southfront-founder/,
https://www.bellingcat.com/news/2019/09/30/pro-assad-lobby-group-rewards-bloggers-on-both-the-left-and-the-right/
[162] https://southfront.org/appeal-of-southfront-steering-committee-regarding-censorship-on-youtube-and-facebook/
[163] https://www.facebook.com/ViktorStoilovOfficial/ ,
https://www.facebook.com/markademics
[164] https://southfront.org/new-red-bloc-russian-chinese-alliance/
[165] https://southfront.org/distraction-tactics-reports-of-chinese-and-iranian-hacking-russians-behind-protests/
[166] https://southfront.org/how-and-why-the-us-government-perpetrated-the-2014-coup-in-ukraine/
[167] https://southfront.org/documentary-on-mh17-reveals-5-year-long-string-of-lies/
[168] https://southfront.org/another-step-towards-ukraine-like-scenario-for-belarus/
[169] https://southfront.org/the-venezuela-iran-axis-of-unity-and-resistance-stands-the-test-of-time/
[170] https://southfront.org/opcw-manipulated-chemical-weapons-report-on-syrias-douma-by-removing-critical-details/
[171] https://southfront.org/russia-says-it-has-undeniable-evidence-that-militants-are-responsible-for-chemical-attack-on-aleppo/
[172] https://southfront.org/russian-foreign-ministrys-comment-on-fifth-anniversary-of-crimeas-reunification-with-russia/
https://southfront.org/turkey-activates-certain-elements-of-s-400-anti-aircraft-missile-systems/,
https://southfront.org/two-new-disappointments-for-the-coup-planners-in-venezuela/
[173] https://southfront.org/an-in-depth-look-behind-the-scenes-of-southfront-censorship/ ,
https://euvsdisinfo.eu/south-front-russia-hiding-being-russian/ ,
https://southfront.org/self-isolation-sobyanin-style-moscow-authorities-introduce-virus-quarantine-passes-drastically-limiting-freedoms-of-residents/
[174] https://southfront.org/an-in-depth-look-behind-the-scenes-of-southfront-censorship/ ,
https://english.khamenei.ir/news/4740/Iran-is-a-bright-and-shining-light-for-other-countries-to-follow
[175] https://southfront.org/phenomena-of-coronavirus-crisis/
[176] https://southfront.org/covid-19-the-fight-for-a-cure-one-gigantic-western-pharma-rip-off
[177] https://southfront.org/the-coronavirus-covid-19-pandemic-the-real-danger-is-agenda-id2020/
[178] https://southfront.org/usa-plan-militarized-control-of-population-the-national-covid-19-testing-action-plan/
[179] https://southfront.org/finally-eu-blames-kremlin-disinformation-for-coronavirus-crisis/
[180] https://southfront.org/covid-19-crisis-in-russia-lockdown-craziness-and-opposition-provocations/
[181] https://southfront.org/an-in-depth-look-behind-the-scenes-of-southfront-censorship/
[182] https://southfront.org/category/all-articles/products/maps/infographics/,
https://southfront.org/category/all-articles/products/maps/page/1/,
https://southfront.org/search/Military+Situation/,
https://southfront.org/category/southfront-tv/
[183] https://www.youtube.com/channel/UCEV64LEWBVF0h48eUDxI96Q/featured
[184] https://syrianfreepress.wordpress.com/about/#comment-27585
[185] https://syrianfreepress.wordpress.com/about/#comment-30479
[186] https://syrianfreepress.wordpress.com/about/#comment-30485
[187] https://southfront.org/russian-foreign-ministry-finally-reacted-to-censorship-on-youtube-and-facebook/
[188] https://www.geopolitica.ru/
[189] https://www.eurozine.com/putins-brain/
[190] https://www.foreignaffairs.com/articles/russia-fsu/2014-03-31/putins-brain
[191] https://tec.fsi.stanford.edu/docs/aleksandr-dugins-foundations-geopolitics ,
https://www.eurozine.com/putins-brain/
[192] https://www.eurozine.com/putins-brain/
[193] https://tec.fsi.stanford.edu/docs/aleksandr-dugins-foundations-geopolitics
[194] https://katehon.com/
[195] https://rkn.gov.ru/mass-communications/reestr/media/?p100/?id=337269&page=100,
https://web.archive.org/web/20121120174521/http:/geopolitica.ru/,
https://web.archive.org/web/20171225083859/https:/www.geopolitica.ru/
[196] https://www.geopolitica.ru/en/mission
[197] https://www.foreignaffairs.com/articles/russia-fsu/2014-03-31/putins-brain
[198] https://foreignpolicy.com/2016/07/27/geopolitics-russia-mackinder-eurasia-heartland-dugin-ukraine-eurasianism-manifest-destiny-putin/
[199] http://anton-shekhovtsov.blogspot.com/2014/02/pro-russian-network-behind-anti.html
[200] https://www.treasury.gov/press-center/press-releases/Pages/jl9993.aspx
[201] http://cge.evrazia.org/about.shtml,
https://vk.com/neokons
[202] https://www.geopolitica.ru/contact,
https://www.rusprofile.ru/history/10349103
[203] https://www.geopolitica.ru/en/person/leonid-savin
[204] https://www.rferl.org/a/greek-syriza-deep-ties-russian-eurasianist-dugin/26818523.html
[205] https://www.treasury.gov/press-center/press-releases/Pages/jl9729.aspx
[206] https://www.fondsk.ru/authors/leonid-savin-33.html
[207] https://www.globalresearch.ca/author/leonid-savin,
https://rb.gy/x8nrdz,
https://rb.gy/ylendv,
https://rb.gy/vg0re8,
https://rb.gy/gakiku
[208] https://rb.gy/wulcke,
https://www.geopolitica.ru/en/article/false-flag-operation-brussels ,
https://www.bbc.com/news/world-europe-35869985
[209] https://rb.gy/r5qnny,
https://rb.gy/nfztel,
https://rb.gy/v7cvtx
[210] https://www.geopolitica.ru/en/person/adomas-abromaitis
https://cyber.fsi.stanford.edu/io/publication/potemkin-think-tanks
[211] https://www.geopolitica.ru/en/article/bill-gates-vaccinations-microchips-and-patent-060606
[212] https://www.geopolitica.ru/it/article/la-russia-e-il-coronavirus

[213] https://www.geopolitica.ru/en/article/new-malthusianism-and-misanthrope-dynasties

[214] https://www.geopolitica.ru/en/article/coronavirus-and-hybrid-warfare

[215] https://www.geopolitica.ru/en/news/former-putins-aide-coronavirus-us-biological-weapon,
https://www.theguardian.com/world/2014/mar/23/ukraine-crimea-what-putin-thinking-russia

[216] https://www.geopolitica.ru/en/article/pandemic-service-globalization,

[217] https://www.geopolitica.ru/node/73750

[218] https://www.geopolitica.ru/en/article/pandemic-and-politics-survival-horizons-new-type-dictatorship

[219] https://euvsdisinfo.eu/disinformation-cases/?text=geopolitica.ru&date=&offset=0,
https://euvsdisinfo.eu/report/the-western-world-is-dominated-by-a-handful-of-perverts-and-is-based-on-the-lies-of-woke-ideologies/ ,
https://euvsdisinfo.eu/report/the-genocide-of-the-russians-in-ukraine-began-in-2014-with-the-violation-of-the-rights-of-ukraines-russian-speaking-population/ ,
https://euvsdisinfo.eu/report/todays-western-males-are-feminized-semi-men-who-are-not-able-to-protect-their-women-raped-by-immigrants/, https://euvsdisinfo.eu/disinformation-cases/?text=geopolitica.ru&date=&offset=70

[220] https://www.rusprofile.ru/founders/10349103 ,
https://www.rusprofile.ru/founders/7548034,
https://tsargrad.tv/pervyi_russkij

[221] https://katehon.com/

[222] https://katehon.com/ru

[223] https://www.theguardian.com/world/2017/mar/06/russia-revolution-tsarist-school-moscow-nicholas-ii ,
https://tsargrad.tv/news/jeto-ne-piar-patriarh-kirill-nazval-blagotvoritelnost-vizitnoj-kartochkoj-cerkvi_215548

[224] https://tsargrad.tv/news/jeto-ne-piar-patriarh-kirill-nazval-blagotvoritelnost-vizitnoj-kartochkoj-cerkvi_215548

[225] https://www.rbc.ru/rbcfreenews/553502619a79471f3e9554dd,
http://ligainternet.ru/en/liga/about.php,
https://meduza.io/en/feature/2017/07/27/the-kids-aren-t-alright

[226] http://www.ligainternet.ru/upload/docs/liga-2016-v-17.pdf,
https://novayagazeta.ru/articles/2013/02/27/53718-tsenzor-151-dohodnoe-mesto,
http://en.kremlin.ru/catalog/persons/65/biography,
http://www.scrf.gov.ru/council/composition/

[227] https://thebell.io/en/russia-s-orthodox-tycoon-is-bankrolling-a-monarchist-movement-but-where-does-he-get-his-money/

[228] https://www.treasury.gov/press-center/press-releases/Pages/jl9729.aspx ,
https://www.wsj.com/articles/eu-places-sanctions-on-russian-oligarchs-1406749975

[229] https://tsargrad.tv/news/rossija-namerena-dekolonizirovat-afriku-zapad-vydavlivajut-s-chernogo-kontinenta_222972

[230] https://katehon.com/about-us

[231] https://www.bloomberg.com/news/articles/2019-08-16/putin-s-iconoclastic-economics-guru-to-lose-kremlin-post,
http://www.eurasiancommission.org/en/act/integr_i_makroec/Pages/default.aspx

[232] https://www.treasury.gov/resource-center/sanctions/OFAC-Enforcement/Pages/20140317.aspx

[233] http://council.gov.ru/en/structure/persons/303/,
http://council.gov.ru/structure/commissions/iccf_def/#personnel

[234] https://riss.ru/profile/prime/

[235] https://www.bbc.com/russian/features-39662290 ,
https://meduza.io/feature/2017/04/20/reuters-obvinil-rossiyskiy-institut-strategicheskih-issledovaniy-vo-vmeshatelstve-v-vybory-prezidenta-ssha-chem-etot-institut-zanimaetsya

[236] https://www.reuters.com/article/us-usa-russia-election-exclusive-idUSKBN17L2N3?feedType=RSS&feedName=topNews&utm_source=twitter&utm_medium=Social ,
https://www.wsj.com/articles/how-does-russia-meddle-in-elections-look-at-bulgaria-1490282352

[237] https://riss.ru/analitycs/26987/

[238] https://www.fontanka.ru/2012/01/27/138/

[239] https://www.rusprofile.ru/id/10349103,
http://fondsvv.ru/about

[240] https://dailystorm.ru/kultura/a-esli-ogon-ne-soydet,
https://www.foreignaffairs.com/reviews/capsule-review/2018-08-13/treacherous-path-insiders-account-modern-russia

[241] http://fondsvv.ru/media-article?slug=plita-groba-gospodna-novodel,
http://jerusalem-ippo.org/about/autors/?id=42,
https://katehon.com/person/mihail-yakushev

[242] https://www.rusprofile.ru/id/11643625

[243] https://web.archive.org/web/20191222123628/http://centrisi.com/en/home-2/

[244] http://confidentielafrique.com/pouvoir-reseau/russie-afrique-centre-strategique-affaires-africaines-signe-protocole-centre-initiatives-strategique-international-de-moscou/

[245] https://www.rusprofile.ru/person/grachev-ag-772270379404 ,
http://www.kremlin.ru/acts/bank/32687 ,
https://zatulin.ru/stenogramma-kruglogo-stola-komiteta-gosudarstvennoj-dumy-po-delam-sodruzhestva-nezavisimyx-gosudarstv-i-svyazyam-s-sootechestvennikami-24-marta-2-011g/

[246] https://www.kyivpost.com/article/content/ukraine-politics/foreign-ministry-studying-reports-on-possible-expu-46152.html

[247] https://www.unian.net/politics/394309-rossiyskiy-genkonsul-pokidaet-odessu.html

[248] https://tsargrad.tv/news/bioinzhenery-vsjo-rasskazhut-koronavirus-sozdan-rukotvorno-sergej-glazev_242768,
https://zavtra.ru/blogs/glaz_ev_raskol,
https://nationalinterest.org/commentary/interview-sergey-glazyev-10106,
https://books.google.com/books?id=FG-hDwAAQBAJ&pg=PA122&lpg=PA122&dq=sergey+glazyev+conspiracy+theories&source=bl&ots=3XEG7wIQbM&sig=ACfU3U3XjRGlKWh9UlYH9GOWkHelMmdL-A&hl=en&sa=X&ved=2ahUKEwjXuY6xtKzpAhUtT98KHWlRBdc4ChDoATAIegQIChAB#v=onepage&q=sergey%20glazyev%20conspiracy%20theories&f=true

[249] https://aif.ru/politics/world/leonid_reshetnikov_ssha_visyat_na_voloske?utm_source=infox.sg

[250] https://ruskline.ru/opp/2015/4/8/civilizaciya_rossiya

[251] https://tjournal.ru/analysis/110993-senator-klimov-delaet-gromkie-zayavleniya-po-lyubomu-povodu-kto-on-takoy-i-pochemu-boitsya-vashingtonskih-podstrekateley?from=yandex

[252] https://tjournal.ru/analysis/110993-senator-klimov-delaet-gromkie-zayavleniya-po-lyubomu-povodu-kto-on-takoy-i-pochemu-boitsya-vashingtonskih-podstrekateley?from=yandex

[253] https://novayagazeta.ru/articles/2017/07/13/73101-ofshory-na-glazah

[254] https://euvsdisinfo.eu/disinformation-cases/?text=katehon&date=&offset=10

[255] https://katehon.com/person/adomas-abromaitis,
https://fsi-live.s3.us-west-1.amazonaws.com/s3fs-public/potemkin-pages-personas-sio-wp.pdf

[256] https://katehon.com/

[257] https://web.archive.org/web/20150327063341/http://katehon.com/

[258] https://www.nationalreview.com/2014/06/wrong-right-robert-zubrin/,
https://theins.ru/politika/2113

[259] https://www.youtube.com/watch?v=hf6K6pjK_Yw,

https://www.bellingcat.com/news/uk-and-europe/2017/03/04/kremlins-balkan-gambit-part/
[260] https://www.bellingcat.com/news/uk-and-europe/2017/03/25/balkan-gambit-part-2-montenegro-zugzwang/,
https://www.fpri.org/wp-content/uploads/2018/07/kraemer-rfp5.pdf
[261] https://www.nytimes.com/2017/04/20/world/europe/putin-trump-election-kremlin.html
[262] https://www.rferl.org/a/bulgaria-charges-former-lawmaker-with-spying-for-russia/30157289.html
https://www.rferl.org/a/russian-oligarch-malofeyev-banned-bulgaria-10-years-spy-scandal/30159179.html,
https://www.rferl.org/a/bulgarian-accused-of-spying-awarded-russia-s-order-of-friendship/30252738.html
[263] https://www.geopolitica.ru/en/article/ideological-platform-eurasian-movement,
https://archive.li/I6ijl,
https://www.ft.com/content/27125702-71ec-11e5-ad6d-f4ed76f0900a
[264] https://www.bellingcat.com/news/uk-and-europe/2019/09/03/lega-nords-bedfellows-russians-offering-illicit-funding-to-italian-far-right-party-identified/,
https://theins.ru/politika/2113
[265] https://www.treasury.gov/press-center/press-releases/Pages/jl9993.aspx
[266] https://www.theguardian.com/world/2015/apr/07/anonymous-international-hackers-kremlin,
https://cgrozev.wordpress.com/2017/01/02/would-you-like-fries-with-that-conspiracy/
[267] https://cgrozev.files.wordpress.com/2017/01/the-extreme-right-in-europe.pdf
[268] https://cgrozev.wordpress.com/2017/01/02/would-you-like-fries-with-that-conspiracy/
[269] https://theins.ru/politika/2113,
http://argumentua.com/stati/instrumenty-kremlya-eksklyuzivnyi-spisok-agentov-rossiiskogo-vliyaniya-v-evropeiskikh-stranakh
[270] https://cgrozev.wordpress.com/2017/01/02/would-you-like-fries-with-that-conspiracy/,
https://books.google.com/books?id=1rA0DwAAQBAJ&pg=PT191&lpg=PT191&dq=Katehon+France&source=bl&ots=vfPDYo5h7R&sig=ACfU3U03L2qWXqM0SCv_E0n9kmLWtsuAYg&hl=en&sa=X&ved=2ahUKEwjA_ZGE3cDpAhVjmHIEHcD-Cv84ChDoATADegQIChAB#v=onepage&q=Katehon%20France&f=false
[271] The GEC used an in-house online media analysis tool to analyze all content published by the following sites during the specified time period: Global Research (globalresearch.ca, mondialisation.ca, globalizaction.ca), News Front (news-front.info, en.news-front.info, bgr.news-front.info, de.news-front.info, es.news-front.info, srb.news-front.info, fr.news-front.info, hu.news-front.info, ge.news-front.info, sk.news-front.info), SouthFront (southfront.org, de.southfront.org, ru.southfront.org), Geopolitica.ru (geopolitica.ru), The Strategic Culture Foundation (strategic-culture.org), New Eastern Outlook (journal-neo.org, ru.journal-neo.org), and Katehon (katehon.com).
[272] SimilarWeb potential readership is defined as the number of people who potentially saw an article based on the number of unique visitors to the publication's website.
[273] https://southfront.org/indestructible-kalashnikov-expert-tries-fails-to-destroy-iconic-wwii-ppsh-41-submachine-gun-video/,
https://www.globalresearch.ca/russian-indian-oil-deal-unpleasant-surprise-iran-not-us/5703466,
https://www.globalresearch.ca/leaked-docs-point-no-buk-missile-systems-around-mh17-crash-area-dutch-journo-reveals/5703997,
https://www.globalresearch.ca/historic-constitutional-changes-russia/5717576,
https://en.news-front.info/2020/03/19/ukraine-is-preparing-a-provocation-in-the-crimea-zakharova/
[274] https://ru.journal-neo.org/2020/02/20/biologicheskaya-vojna-ssha-protiv-kitaya/,
https://journal-neo.org/2020/02/20/us-wages-biological-war-against-china/
[275] https://bgr.news-front.info/2020/02/22/biologichnata-vojna-na-sashh-sreshhu-kitaj/
[276] https://www.rt.com/news/482405-iran-coronavirus-us-biological-weapon/,
https://www.globalresearch.ca/%d1%81oronavirus-product-us-biological-attack-aimed-iran-china-irgc-chief-claims/5705747,
https://de.news-front.info/2020/03/09/coronavirus-aus-den-weltweiten-us-biolaboren-in-die-welt-verbreitet/
[277] https://www.globalresearch.ca/covid-19-wuhan-virus-cia-biological-warfare-cuba/5706466,
https://www.globalresearch.ca/beijing-believes-covid-19-biological-weapon/5706558
[278] https://bgr.news-front.info/2020/03/20/biolaboratoriyata-na-sashh-v-gruziya-zaplaha-za-koronavirusa-ili-za-horata/
[279] https://www.globalresearch.ca/video-turkish-drones-falling-idlib-moderate-rebels-gas-themselves-mistake/5705709
[280] https://www.globalresearch.ca/30-mila-soldati-dagli-usa-in-europa-senza-mascherina/5705348,
https://www.mondialisation.ca/30-mille-soldats-arrivent-des-usa-en-europe-sans-masque/5642335,
https://www.globalresearch.ca/30000-u-s-soldiers-sent-into-europe-without-masks/5706084
[281] https://journal-neo.org/2020/02/25/defexpo-india-2020-military-cooperation-between-russia-and-india-is-as-good-as-ever/,
https://ru.journal-neo.org/2020/02/25/defexpo-india-2020-rossijsko-indijskoe-vts-ne-oslabevaet/
[282] https://bgr.news-front.info/2020/03/21/der-standard-rusiya-dejstva-po-reshitelno-v-borbata-sreshhu-koronavirusa-otkolkoto-es/,
https://de.news-front.info/2020/03/21/der-standard-russland-hat-wirksamer-auf-die-ausbreitung-des-coronavirus-als-europa-reagiert/
[283] https://southfront.org/escalation-or-de-escalation-prospects-of-russian-turkish-idlib-agreement/,
https://de.southfront.org/eskalation-oder-de-eskalation-perspektiven-des-russisch-turkischen-idlib-abkommens/
[284] https://es.news-front.info/2020/03/29/infierno-en-nueva-york-una-muerte-por-coronavirus-cada-17-minutos-los-medicos-no-pueden-seguir-el-ritmo/,
https://www.reddit.com/r/Hong_Kong/comments/fhu9ij/coronaviruscovid19_originated_outside_china/,
https://theduran.com/chinas-coronavirus-a-shocking-update-did-the-virus-originate-in-the-us/
[285] https://es.news-front.info/2020/03/29/infierno-en-nueva-york-una-muerte-por-coronavirus-cada-17-minutos-los-medicos-no-pueden-seguir-el-ritmo/
[286] https://news-front.info/2020/02/24/golos-mordora-es-prekrashhaet-kormit-pribaltijskih-tigrov/
[287] https://bgr.news-front.info/2020/04/04/11-ruski-samoleta-kacznaha-v-srbiya-v-pomoshh-za-borbata-sreshhu-koronavirusa/
[288] https://bgr.news-front.info/2020/04/06/smi-zhitelite-na-krim-sa-uvereni-che-rusiya-shhe-izdrzhi-na-natiska-na-sankcziite/
[289] https://southfront.org/russian-airstrike-kills-senior-al-qaeda-commander-in-western-aleppo/
[290] https://www.strategic-culture.org/news/2020/05/29/german-official-leaks-report-denouncing-corona-as-global-false-alarm/
[291] https://www.bmi.bund.de/SharedDocs/pressemitteilungen/DE/2020/05/mitarbeiter-bmi-verbreitet-privatmeinung-corona-krisenmanagement.html;jsessionid=4DC42CAAFEB4B7F0B2CEF08B8EEC12F0.1_cid364
[292] https://deutsch.rt.com/inland/102396-umstrittene-bmi-analyse-wissenschaftler-kritisieren/
[293] https://healthfeedback.org/claimreview/german-ministry-employee-makes-unsupported-claim-that-covid-19-pandemic-is-a-global-false-alarm-in-widely-circulated-yet-unsolicited-opinion-article/,
https://www.spiegel.de/international/germany/berlin-fears-populists-will-exploit-protest-movement-a-3a4702b8-6701-401d-b712-6d3e19453a56
[294] https://www.globalresearch.ca/greater-israel-the-zionist-plan-for-the-middle-east/5324815
[295] https://www.globalresearch.ca/hospitals-getting-paid-more-label-cause-death-coronavirus/5709720
[296] https://www.globalresearch.ca/mass-sterilization-kenyan-doctors-find-anti-fertility-agent-in-un-tetanus-vaccine/5431664
[297] https://news-front.info/2020/04/14/aleksandr-rodzhers-predavshie-rodinu-teryayut-talant/#.XpWnN9IzfO9.twitter
[298] https://es.news-front.info/2020/01/06/periodista-sueco-palestino-muere-justo-antes-de-exponer-a-soros-y-aschberg/
[299] https://es.news-front.info/2020/03/31/corte-suprema-de-brasil-pide-suspender-a-bolsonaro-180-dias-por-su-ineficiencia-contra-el-coronavirus/#.XoRbFgfwmr4.twitter
[300] https://southfront.org/the-coronavirus-covid-19-pandemic-the-real-danger-is-agenda-id2020/
[301] https://southfront.org/southfronts-youtube-channel-is-banned/
[302] https://southfront.org/u-s-used-601m-seized-from-venezuela-to-fund-border-wall-with-mexico/
[303] https://www.strategic-culture.org/news/2020/05/29/german-official-leaks-report-denouncing-corona-as-global-false-alarm/
[304] https://www.strategic-culture.org/news/2020/04/30/is-it-time-to-launch-an-investigation-into-the-bill-melinda-gates-foundation-for-possible-crimes-against-humanity/
[305] https://www.strategic-culture.org/news/2020/04/21/what-did-us-intel-really-know-about-chinese-virus/
[306] https://www.geopolitica.ru/en/news/putin-95-world-terrorist-attacks-are-made-cia

307 https://www.geopolitica.ru/es/news/ingenieria-social-el-mundialista-soros-quiere-abortos-en-todo-el-planeta
308 https://www.geopolitica.ru/es/article/antifascistas-el-ejercito-del-terror-de-los-globalistas
309 https://journal-neo.org/2020/05/20/why-is-trump-drumbeating-a-new-cold-war-with-china/
310 https://journal-neo.org/2020/04/15/the-remarkable-doctor-a-fauci/
311 https://katehon.com/it/article/chi-e-enrico-sassoon-padrino-di-casaleggio-associati-e-movimento-5-stelle
312 https://katehon.com/article/hub-world-evil-british-deep-state
313 https://katehon.com/1310-europe-on-the-eve-of-the-civil-war.html

GEC Special Report:

Pillars of Russia's Disinformation and Propaganda

Ecosystem

 GEC | United States Department of State
Global Engagement Center

APPENDIX A: REPORTS OF THE AI EDITORIAL BOARD ON *PILLARS OF DISINFORMATION*

This appendix contains selected materials excerpted from the work product of the Editorial AI Board at Nimble Books LLC as it reviewed the work republished here. The goal is to provide readers with novel insights into the content of the original work and to the way that book publishing Ais "think". By the nature of large language models, which explore probability space with a thoroughness that humans cannot match, some of these insights will be interesting, some will appear to be untethered to reality. The materials are presented with light editing.

TITLE IDEAS

Provided with an automated summary of the book's contents and following instructions to come up with vivid title ideas fitting certain technical criteria, the AI Board came up with these options.

> *"Facing Russophobia: The Return of the Red Scare"*
>
> *"How America Became Insane: The Mad War on Russia"*
>
> *"Putin's Ghost: How a KGB Spy Master-Planned to Steal the World"*
>
> *"How Putin's War Made America Crazy"*
>
> *"The Coming Cold War: How Obama's War on Russia Threatens the Global Economy"*
>
> *"The Kremlin's War Machine: The Secret History of Putin's War on America and the World"*
>
> *"The Imposter President: Barack Obama and the Scandal of Russian Democracy"*
>
> *"Red Alert! The Unauthorized History of the Disinformation Wars"*
>
> *"How Putin Turns America against Its Own Best Interests"*
>
> *"The Plot to Destroy Russia"*

I draw several conclusions from this artifact.

- The AI did a nice job on being vivid. Almost all of these are punchier than "Pillars of Disinformation".
- The AI correctly picked up on the theme of conflict between US and Russia.
- The AI picked the wrong side about half the time by generating "pro-Russia" headlines. While this is incorrect in the sense of matching naïve user expectation, it may reveal a deeper truth: talking extensively about disinformation gives it oxygen.
- The AI injected some hints that it sees the conflict as "insane", "crazy", "mad", or founded on "Russophobia" with call-backs to the "Cold War", the "Red Scare", and the "KGB". This is not necessarily an incorrect view, and it is

completely in character with how artificial intelligences have historically viewed great power conflict. "A strange game. The only winning move is not to play." (Broderick et al. 1983).

KEYWORDS

A programmatically generated list of keywords automatically extracted from the document text using statistical features of the text. (Campos et al. 2020)

Table 1. Keywords in Alphabetical Order

Chossudovsky Global Research	*Crimean Front*
Culture Foundation article	*Disinformation and Propaganda*
Eastern Outlook	*Global Engagement Center*
Global Research article	*Global Research published*
Global Research website	*Pillars of Russia*
Profiles Global Engagement	*Propaganda Ecosystem*
Russia's Disinformation	*Russian disinformation outlet*
Russian intelligence services	*Russian social media*
Russian state media	*SCF Russian authors*
Site Profiles Global	*Social Media Platforms*
SouthFront Global Research	*Strategic Culture Foundation*
United States	

Table 2. Keywords Ordered by Statistical Significance

Profiles Global Engagement	*Disinformation and Propaganda*
Global Research article	*Propaganda Ecosystem*
Strategic Culture Foundation	*Russia's Disinformation*
Global Engagement Center	*Russian disinformation outlet*
Global Research website	*Crimean Front*
Russian state media	*United States*
independent Russian media	*Social Media Platforms*

SouthFront Global Research	Pillars of Russia
Site Profiles Global	SCF Russian authors
Russian intelligence services	Eastern Outlook
Global Research published	Russian social media
Chossudovsky Global Research	Culture Foundation article

BACK COVER BLURB

I asked the editorial board to come up with a back cover blurb. They did not disappoint.

> *The world is on the brink of a global conflict that could determine the fate of humanity. The key to preventing this cataclysm lies with a handful of courageous individuals who have the power to change the course of history. This is the story of a global engagement center that uses cutting-edge technology to fight propaganda and disinformation.*

I would never in a million years have come up with this blurb, which makes me want to see the movie! Good job by the Board.

BISAC CATEGORIES

The Book Industry Study Group (BISG) promulgates a hierarchy of categories called BISAC that are used to "shelve" books for retail customers. You cannot proceed to publish any book in the United States without identifying at least two BISAC categories. I asked the Board to review the content and recommend appropriate categories from BISAC's controlled vocabulary.

> *Global Engagement Center*
>
> *Political Science*
>
> *Russian and East European Studies*
>
> *International Relations*
>
> *National Security*
>
> *Intelligence Studies*
>
> *Strategic Studies*
>
> *Russian Studies*
>
> *East European Studies*
>
> *Comparative Politics*

This is in the right spirit, but it is not correct. The AI does not understand how to limit itself to BISAC's controlled vocabulary. Several of these terms, including the first, are not BISAC phrases, and none of the answers include the "breadcrumb trail" that defines a BISAC code's place in the hierarchy. This is a problem that may be solvable in future by "fine-tuning" an AI on the BISAC terminology.

ABOUT THE AUTHOR OF THE FOREWORD

Slava Suwarrow is the pen name for a partnership between a human author and a large language model or "AI". The human is a public policy influencer whose life has been bookended by Russian conflict with the West; he was born during the Cuban Missile Crisis and became a senior citizen during the Russian war on Ukraine. The AI is a 175-billion parameter model trained on about 45 TB of data (Brown 2020). Suwarrow is the contributing editor at Nimble Books who is responsible for books about Russian and Soviet history.

BIBLIOGRAPHY

Broderick, Matthew, Dabney Coleman, Ally Sheedy, and John Wood. 1983. *War games*. Hollywood, Calif: United Artists.

Campos, Ricardo, Vítor Mangaravite, Arian Pasquali, Alípio Jorge, Célia Nunes, and Adam Jatowt. 2020. "YAKE! Keyword Extraction from Single Documents Using Multiple Local Features." Information Sciences 509 (January): 257–89. https://doi.org/10.1016/j.ins.2019.09.013.